DR. STOCKMANN'S HOUSE

EDITORIAL OFFICE

ROOM IN THE CAPTAIN'S HOUSE

Photos by Alfredo Valente

AN ENEMY OF THE PEOPLE

by Henrik Ibsen

ACTING EDITION

BY HENRIK IBSEN

AN ADAPTATION FOR THE AMERICAN STAGE

BY ARTHUR MILLER

DRAMATISTS
PLAY SERVICE
INC.

AN ENEMY OF THE PEOPLE
Copyright © Renewed 1979, Arthur Miller
Copyright © 1950, 1951, Arthur Miller

Arthur Miller's adaptation of AN ENEMY OF THE PEOPLE by Henrik Ibsen was first presented by Lars Nordenson at the Broadhurst Theatre in New York on December 28, 1950. It was directed by Robert Lewis, setting and costumes were by Aline Bernstein, and lighting was by Charles Elson.

THE CAST WAS AS FOLLOWS:

MORTEN KIIL	Art Smith
BILLING	Michael Strong
CATHERINE STOCKMANN	Florence Eldridge
PETER STOCKMANN	Morris Carnovsky
HOVSTAD	Martin Brooks
DR. STOCKMANN	Fredric March
MORTEN	Ralph Robertson
EJLIF	Richard Trask
CAPTAIN HORSTER	Ralph Dunn
PETRA	Anna Minot
ASLAKSEN	Fred Stewart
THE DRUNK	Lou Gilbert

TOWNSPEOPLE: Lulla Adler, Barbara Ames, Paul Fitzpatrick, James Karen, Michael Lewin, Salem Ludwig, Gene Lyons, John Marley, Arnold Schulman, Robert Simon, Rod Steiger

The action takes place in a Norwegian town.

Act I

SCENE 1: Dr. Stockmann's living room.

SCENE 2: The same, the following morning.

Act II

SCENE 1: Editorial office of the *People's Daily Messenger.*

SCENE 2: A room in Captain Horster's house.

Act III

SCENE: Dr. Stockmann's living room the following morning.

In Act II, Scene 2, there are several bit parts.[1] The following have a few lines each:

Nansen	Tora	Gunnar
Edvard	Finn	Knut
Georg	Henrik	Gabriel
Paul	Hedvig	Hans

Of the above mentioned characters, Hedvig and Tora are women.

---

[1] These characters were not indicated in the original program.

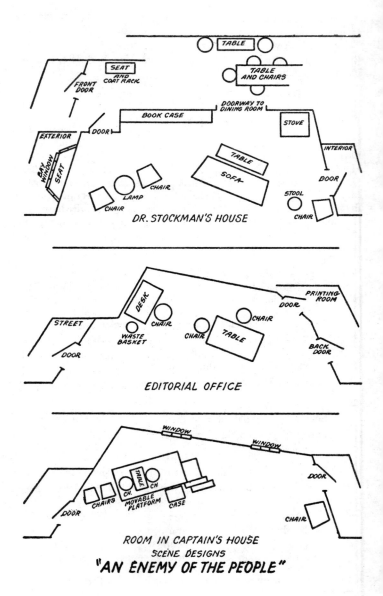

DR. STOCKMAN'S HOUSE

EDITORIAL OFFICE

ROOM IN CAPTAIN'S HOUSE
SCENE DESIGNS
"AN ENEMY OF THE PEOPLE"

4

AN ENEMY OF THE PEOPLE

ACT I

SCENE 1

It is evening. DR. STOCKMANN'S *living-room is simply but cheerfully furnished. A doorway* U. R. *leads into the entrance hall, which extends from the front door to the dining-room. Only a small part of the hallway is seen* U. R., *but there is a passageway extending back-stage from the front door to the dining-room. This dining-room will be described below. The point is that the passageway is practical for actors, but unseen by the audience. There is a doorway or archway* U. L. *which leads into the dining-room. Just inside this doorway we see the* R. *end of a dining-room table. There is one dining-room chair downstage, one at* R. *of the table and two just above. A short distance up-stage of the end of the table that is visible to the audience is a sideboard or table with one chair on each side of it. The* R. *end of the dining-room table, the one visible to the audience, stands about halfway between* R. *and* L. *side of the sideboard or table. Down* L., *about two-thirds of the way to the curtain-line, is another door which leads into* STOCK-MANN'S *study and other rooms of the house.* U. L., *fitting into the corner of the room, is a tiled stove. Somewhat below this and to* R., *is a sofa with a table behind it.* D. L. *below door is an armchair, and near it another small chair. In* R. *foreground, somewhat to* R. *of* C., *are two chairs, a small table between them, on which stand a lamp and a bowl of apples. A bay window is in* R. *wall about halfway down-stage, and immediately below this is a bench or window seat.*

5

As the curtain rises KIIL *is busily eating in the dining room.* BILLING *is watching him.* KIIL *quickly rises and goes around* BILLING *to his coat and hat which are lying on upstage end of sofa.*

BILLING. (*Following him.*) You sure eat fast, Mr. Kiil!

KIIL. Eating don't get you anywhere, boy. (BILLING *helps him with his coat.*) Tell my daughter I went home.

BILLING. All right. (*He returns to dining-room and begins to eat.* KIIL *crosses to* D. R. *of* R. C. *table, sees apple, stops, takes it, bites it, likes it, takes another, which he puts into his pocket. Starts toward door* U. R. *but circles back to table and takes a third apple, which he puts into his pocket. He notices tobacco humidor on table, looks slyly up at dining-room, comes* D. *to* L. *of table and covertly fills his coat pocket with tobacco. As he sets the humidor down,* CATHERINE *enters* D. L. KIIL *starts off* U. R. CATHERINE *starts to put on apron.*)

CATHERINE. (*Crosses* D. C.) Father! You're not going, are you?

KIIL. Got all kinds of business to tend to.

CATHERINE. Oh, you're only going to sit alone in your room and you know it! Stay—Mr. Billing's here, and Mr. Hovstad's coming; it'll be interesting for you.

KIIL. No, I got all kinds of business. Only reason I come over was the butcher told me you bought roast beef today. And it was very tasty, dear.

CATHERINE. Why don't you wait for Tom? He only went for a little walk.

KIIL. (*Points to tobacco can on table.*) You suppose he'd mind if I filled my pipe?

CATHERINE. Oh, help yourself! (*He does so.*) And why don't you take some apples? (*Offering him bowl of apples.*) You should always have some fruit in your room, go ahead.

KIIL. No, no, wouldn't think of it.

CATHERINE. Why don't you move in with us, Father? I often wonder if you're eating.

KIIL. I'm eating. Well . . . (*Doorbell rings* U. R.) See you soon, Catherine.

CATHERINE. (*Crosses* U. C. *to door* U. R.) That must be Hovstad. (KIIL *steps* R. *and lights his pipe.*)

PETER. (*Entering hall.*) Good evening, Catherine. How are you tonight? (*Sees* KIIL.) Mr. Kiil!

KIIL. Your Honor! (*Takes big bite out of apple and goes out* U. R.)

CATHERINE. You mustn't mind him, Peter. He's getting terribly old. Wouldn't you like some supper?

PETER STOCKMANN. (*Sees* BILLING *who has stepped into dining-room archway and given a suggestion of a salute.*) No . . . no, thanks.

CATHERINE. (*Nervously, quietly.*) He just sort of dropped by, Peter.

PETER. (CATHERINE *has taken his coat and hangs it up in* U. R. *hall.*) That's all right. I can't take hot food in the evening, any-way. I stick to my tea and toast. Much healthier and more economical.

CATHERINE. (*Smiling.*) You sound as though Tom and I threw money out the window.

PETER. (*Crossing* D. C., *looks* U. *and then to* D. L. *door.*) Not you, Catherine. He wouldn't be home, would he?

CATHERINE. (*Following him.*) He went for a little walk with the boys.

PETER. You don't think that's dangerous—right after dinner? (*Loud knocking on door.* CATHERINE *crosses* U. R. *to door.*) That sounds like my brother. (PETER *crosses* R. C.)

CATHERINE. Tom? He hasn't knocked on the door for ten years. (HOVSTAD *enters* U. R., *coat and hat in hand.*) Mr. Hovstad! Come in, please.

HOVSTAD. (*Handing her hat and coat, then crossing* D. R. *to* R. *of* PETER. CATHERINE *hangs up clothes in hallway* U. R.) Sorry I'm late. I was held up at the printing shop. (*A little surprised.*) Good evening, Your Honor. (CATHERINE *crosses* U. *around* R. *table to* L. *of* PETER.)

PETER. (*Sitting in* R. C. *chair.*) Hovstad. On business, no doubt.

HOVSTAD. Partly. It's about an article for the paper . . .

PETER. Ha! I didn't doubt it. I understand my brother has become a very prolific contributor to—what do you call it—(*Sarcas-tically.*) *The People's Daily Liberator?*

HOVSTAD. (*Holding his ground. Crosses* PETER.) *The People's Daily Messenger*, sir? (*Turning to* PETER.) The Doctor sometimes honors the *Messenger* when he wants to uncover the real truth of some subject.

7

PETER. The truth. Oh, yes, I see . . .

CATHERINE. (*Nervously crossing* D. *to* HOVSTAD.) Would you like to . . . (*Points to dining-room.*)

HOVSTAD. No, thanks.

PETER. I don't want you to think I blame the Doctor for using your columns. After all, every performer goes for the audience that applauds him most. It's really not your paper I have anything against, Mr. Hovstad. (CATHERINE *busies herself with little house-work things on sofa table, crossing from* D. *end of sofa to* U. *end.*)

HOVSTAD. I really didn't think so, Your Honor.

PETER. As a matter of fact, I happen to admire the spirit of toler-ance in our town—it's magnificent. Just don't forget that we have it because we all believe in the same thing; it brings us together.

HOVSTAD. Kirsten Springs, you mean?

PETER. The Springs, Mr. Hovstad, our wonderful new Springs. They've changed the soul of this town. Mark my words, Kirsten Springs are going to put us on the map, and there's no question about it.

CATHERINE. (*Moving* U. C. *of sofa table.*) That's what Tom says, too.

PETER. Everything is shooting ahead; real estate going up, money changing hands every hour, business humming . . .

HOVSTAD. And no more unemployment.

PETER. Right. Give us a really good summer and sick people will be coming here in carloads, the Springs will turn into a regular fad, a new Carlsbad. And for once, the well-to-do people won't be the only ones paying taxes in this town.

HOVSTAD. I hear reservations are really starting to come in?

PETER. Coming in every day. Looks very promising, very promis-ing.

HOVSTAD. That's fine. (*To* CATHERINE.) Then the Doctor's article will come in handy.

PETER. He's written something again?

HOVSTAD. No, it's a piece he wrote during the winter recommend-ing the water. But at the time, I let the article lie . . .

PETER. Why, some hitch in it?

HOVSTAD. Oh, no, I just thought it would have a bigger effect in the spring, when people start planning for the summer.

PETER. That's smart, Mr. Hovstad, very smart.

CATHERINE. (*Crossing D. to L. of* HOVSTAD.) Tom is always so full of ideas about the Springs; every day he . . .

PETER. Well, he ought to be, he gets his salary from the Springs, my dear.

HOVSTAD. Oh, I think it's more than that, don't you? Doctor Stockmann *created* Kirsten Springs.

PETER. (*Looks at* HOVSTAD.) You don't say! I've been hearing that lately, but I did think I had a certain modest part . . .

CATHERINE. Oh, Tom always says . . .

HOVSTAD. I only meant the original idea was . . .

PETER. (*Rises, crosses D. L.*) My good brother is never at a loss for ideas. All sorts of ideas. But when it comes to putting them into action you need another kind of man, and I did think that at least people in this house would . . .

CATHERINE. But, Peter, dear . . . we didn't mean to . . . (*To* HOVSTAD, *helping him off stage toward dining-room a little.*) Go get yourself a bite, Mr. Hovstad, my husband will be here any minute.

HOVSTAD. (*Overlapping a little.*) Thank you, maybe just a little something . . . (*Enters dining-room through* U. L. *doorway, sits in* D. *chair.*)

PETER. (*Lowering his voice.*) Isn't it remarkable . . . Why is it that people without background can never learn tact?

CATHERINE. Why upset yourself, Peter? Can't you and Thomas share the honor, like good brothers?

PETER. The trouble is that certain men are never satisfied to share, Catherine.

CATHERINE. Nonsense. You've always gotten along beautifully with Tom . . . (DOCTOR THOMAS STOCKMANN, MORTEN, EJLIF *and* CAPTAIN HORSTER *are heard approaching.* CATHERINE *crosses up to hall* U. R.) That must be him now. (STOCKMANN, HORSTER *and the boys,* EJLIF *and* MORTEN, *enter* U. R. *joking and laughing, about racing each other home.*)

STOCKMANN. (*Taking off coat, revealing smoking-jacket underneath.*) Hey, Catherine! Here's another guest for you! Here's a hanger for your coat, Captain. (*During following,* CATHERINE *is trying to tell* STOCKMANN *about* PETER.)

HORSTER. I don't need . . .

STOCKMANN. Oh, that's right, you don't wear overcoats! (*Claps* MORTEN *on the behind.* MORTEN *spars a moment.*) Go on in, boys.

9

You kids must be hungry all over again. (*Boys exit* U. R. *and appear in dining-room.*) Come here, Captain Horster, I want you to get a look at this roast. (HORSTER *crosses* L. *to dining-room, sits in* U. *chair.*)

CATHERINE. Tom, dear . . . (*Motions toward* PETER.)

STOCKMANN. (*Turns, sees* PETER.) Oh, Peter . . . (*Crosses above* R. *chairs to* PETER, C., *holding out his hand.*) Say, now, this is really nice. (CATHERINE *crosses* D. R. *in front of table.*)

PETER. I'll have to go in a minute.

STOCKMANN. (*Crossing* R. *to* CATHERINE.) Oh, nonsense, not with the toddy on the table. You haven't forgotten the toddy, have you, Catherine? (*Kisses* CATHERINE.)

CATHERINE. (*Crossing* U. *to dining-room.*) Of course not, I've got the water boiling. (*Goes into dining-room, closes portieres.*)

PETER. Toddy, too?!

STOCKMANN. (*Crosses to* PETER, *takes his arm, seats him in* R. C. *chair.*) Sure, just sit down and make yourself at home.

PETER. (*Resisting a little, but sitting.*) No, thanks, I don't go in for drinking parties.

STOCKMANN. (*At* L. *of* PETER.) But this is no party.

PETER. What else do you call it? (*Looks toward dining-room.*) It's extraordinary how you people can consume all this food and live.

STOCKMANN. Why? What's finer than to watch young people eat! (*Nudging* PETER.) Peter, those are the fellows who are going to stir up the whole future.

PETER. Is that so?! What's there to stir up?

STOCKMANN. Don't worry, they'll let us know when the time comes. Old idiots like you and me, we'll be left behind like . . .

PETER. I've never been called *that* before.

STOCKMANN. (*Fixing book in bookcase.*) Oh, Peter, don't jump on me every minute, will you? You know your trouble, Peter— your impressions are blunted. You ought to sit up there in that crooked corner of the North for five years like I did and then come back here. It's like watching the first seven days of Creation.

PETER. Here?!

STOCKMANN. Things to work and fight for, Peter! Without that, you're dead. (*Calling.*) Catherine, are you sure the mailman came today?

CATHERINE. (*From dining-room.*) There wasn't any mail today.

STOCKMANN. (*Crossing to* L. *of* PETER.) And another thing, Peter, a good income; *that's* something you learn to value after you've lived on a starvation diet.

PETER. When did you starve?

STOCKMANN. Damned near! It was pretty tough going a lot of the time up there. And now, to be able to live like a prince—tonight, for instance, we had roast beef for dinner and, by God, there was enough left for supper, too! (*Takes* PETER'S *arm, tries to push him to dining-room.*) Please have a piece—come here.

PETER. (*At* C.) Oh, no, no—please, certainly not.

STOCKMANN. At least, let me show it to you! Come in here, we even have a table-cloth.

PETER. I saw it.

STOCKMANN. (*Offering fruit to* PETER.) Live to the hilt! That's my motto. Anyway, Catherine says I'm earning almost as much as we spend.

PETER. (*Declining fruit.*) Well, you're improving.

STOCKMANN. (*Crossing* PETER U. *to dining-room archway. Looking into dining-room.*) Why can't I give myself the pleasure of having young interesting people around me? You'll see—when Hovstad comes in, we'll talk and . . .

PETER. (*Sitting in* R. C. *chair.*) Oh, yes, Hovstad. That reminds me—he told me he was going to print one of your articles.

STOCKMANN. One of my articles?

PETER. Yes, about the Springs—an article you wrote during the winter.

STOCKMANN. (*Checking his appointment book in front of sofa.*) Oh, that one—in the first place, I don't want that one printed right now.

PETER. No? It sounded to me as though it would be very timely.

STOCKMANN. Under normal conditions maybe so.

PETER. Well, what's abnormal about the conditions now?

STOCKMANN. (*In front of sofa, turns.*) I can't say that for the moment, Peter—at least not tonight. There could be a great deal abnormal about conditions—then again, there could be nothing at all.

PETER. Well, you've managed to sound mysterious. Is there anything wrong? Something you are keeping from me? Because I wish once in a while you'd remind yourself that I am chairman of the board for the Springs, as well as Mayor.

11

ΓOCKMANN. And I'd like you to remember that, Peter. (*Crosses*
D. *behind sofa.*) Look, let's not get into each other's hair.

PETER. For God's sake, no—I don't make a habit of getting into
people's *hair*. But I'd like to underline that everything concerning
Kirsten Springs must be treated in a businesslike manner, through
the proper channels and dealt with by the legally constituted authorities. I can't allow anything done behind my back in a round-
about way.

STOCKMANN. (*Crossing back to* PETER *with bowl of nuts, offering
him some.*) When did I ever go behind your back, Peter?

PETER. (*Declining nuts, but* STOCKMANN *takes some.*) You have
an ingrained tendency to go *your own way*, Thomas, and that simply can't go on in a well-organized society. The individual really
must subordinate himself to the overall—or more accurately (*Indicating self.*) to the authorities who are in charge of the general
welfare.

STOCKMANN. (*Crossing back behind sofa.*) Well, that's probably
so, (*Cracks nut.*) but how the hell does that concern me, Peter?

PETER. (*Rises, crosses* U. *a step.*) My dear Thomas, this is exactly what you will never learn—but you had better watch out
because some day you might pay dearly for it. (*Crosses* U. R. *to
coat in hall* U. R.) Now I've said it—good-bye.

STOCKMANN. Are you out of your mind? (*Follows* PETER U. R. C.
behind table, carrying bowl.) You're absolutely on the wrong
track.

PETER. I am usually not—anyway, may I be excused? (*Nods into
dining-room.*) Good-bye, Catherine. Good evening, gentlemen.
(*He leaves* U. R. *The men mumble farewells.*)

CATHERINE. (*Entering from dining-room.*) He left?

STOCKMANN. (*Surprised at* PETER'S *behavior. Above* R. *chair.*)
Yes, he did, and thoroughly burned up.

CATHERINE. (*At* U. C.) What'd you do to him now?

STOCKMANN. What does he want from me? He can't expect me
to give him an accounting of every move I make—every thought
I think, until I'm ready to do it.

CATHERINE. Why? What should you give him an accounting of?

STOCKMANN. Just leave that to me, Catherine. (*Crosses to bay
window* R., *looking out, setting bowl on window seat.*) It is pe-
culiar that the mailman didn't come today. (CATHERINE *goes to
dining-room. Men enter downstage from dining-room, opening*

12

…res: HORSTER L. of HOVSTAD; HOVSTAD crosses D. to L. of …chair, BILLING in front of D. end of sofa, EJLIF and MORTEN L. chair.)

…NG. *(Stretching out his arms.)* After a meal like that, by …I feel like a new man. This house is so . . .

…AD. *(Cutting him off.)* The Mayor certainly wasn't in a …g mood tonight.

…MANN. It's his stomach—he has a lousy digestion.

HOVSTAD. *(Indicating BILLING and self.)* I think two editors from the *People's Daily Messenger* didn't help, either.

STOCKMANN. No, it's just that Peter is a lonely man—poor fellow, all he knows is official business and duties and then all that damn weak tea that he pours into himself. Catherine, may we have the toddy?

CATHERINE. *(From dining-room.)* I'm just getting it.

STOCKMANN. *(Takes HORSTER to sofa, crossing HOVSTAD and BILLING.)* Sit down here on the couch with me, Captain Horster—a rare guest like you—sit here. Sit down, friends. *(HORSTER sits on D. end of sofa.)*

HORSTER. This used to be such an ugly house; suddenly it's beautiful!

BILLING. *(To HORSTER, intimately, indicating STOCKMANN.)* Great man. *(STOCKMANN, embarrassed, turns to see to whom BILLING refers, sits, BILLING crosses U. around to R. chair, sits. The men rise as CATHERINE brings in from dining-room tray with pot, glasses, three bottles and sets it on table behind sofa, then crosses and sits in L. chair.)*

CATHERINE. *(Entering.)* Here you are. Help yourselves.

STOCKMANN. *(Fixing toddy.)* We sure will. *(EJLIF is tucking in MORTEN'S sweater.)* And the cigars, Ejlif—you know where the box is—and, Morten, get my pipe. *(MORTEN and EJLIF exit L. and EJLIF just overhears STOCKMANN'S suspicions about cigars.)* I have a sneaking suspicion that Ejlif is snitching a cigar now and then, but I don't pay any attention. *(MORTEN re-enters L. and stands on STOCKMANN'S R. with his pipe.)* Catherine, you know where I put it? Oh, he's got it. Good boys! *(EJLIF re-enters L. with cigars, offers them to HORSTER, HOVSTAD and BILLING then sits U. of MORTEN on window seat R. eating nuts from bowl. STOCKMANN gives toddy to HOVSTAD, BILLING and HORSTER then returns to U. of sofa.)* Help yourselves, fellows. I'll stick to the

13

pipe—this one's gone through plenty of blizzards with me up in the north. (*Sits* U. *end of sofa.*) Skol! (BILLING *and* HOVSTAD *clink glasses,* HORSTER *and* STOCKMANN *clink glasses. All drink.* STOCKMANN *looks around.*) Home! (*All look at* STOCKMANN.) What an invention, heh!

CATHERINE. (*After a moment.*) Are you sailing soon, Captain Horster?

HORSTER. I expect to be ready next week.

CATHERINE. And then to America, Captain?

HORSTER. Yes, that's the plan.

BILLING. Oh, then you won't be home for the new election?

HORSTER. Is there going to be another election?

BILLING. Don't you know? (STOCKMANN *lights pipe.*)

HORSTER. No, I don't get mixed up in those things.

BILLING. But you are interested in public affairs, aren't you?

HORSTER. Frankly, I don't understand a thing about it.

CATHERINE. (*Sympathetically.*) Neither do I, Captain; maybe that's why I'm always so glad to see you.

BILLING. Just the same, you ought to vote, Captain.

HORSTER. Even if I don't understand anything about it?

BILLING. Understand? What do you mean by that? Society, Captain, is like a ship—every man should do something to help navigate the ship.

HORSTER. That may be all right on shore, but on board a ship it doesn't work out so well. (PETRA, *carrying hat and coat with textbooks and notepads under her arm, enters from hall* U. R.)

PETRA. Good evening. (*Men rise.* PETRA *removes her coat and hat and places books on hall chair* U. R. *There are mutual greetings.*)

STOCKMANN. (*Warmly.*) Good evening, Petra.

PETRA. (*Crosses* C. *to* STOCKMANN, *throwing kiss to* CATHERINE, *which she throws back.*) And here you are lying around like lizards while I'm out slaving.

STOCKMANN. (*Embracing* PETRA *at* C.) Well, you come and be a lizard, too. (*To company.*) I look at her and I say to myself—how did I do it!

BILLING. (*Close to* HOVSTAD.) Great young woman. (*Crosses to* PETRA.) Shall I mix a toddy for you?

PETRA. Thank you, I had better do it myself—you always mix it too strong. Oh, Father, I forgot—I have a letter for you. (*Goes to hall* U. R., *brings down book with letter in it.*)

STOCKMANN. (*Crosses after her. Alerted, sets drink on table, returns to* C.) Who's it from?

PETRA. (*Takes letter, backs* D. R. *then* C., STOCKMANN *follows her.*) I met the mailman on the way to school this morning and he gave me your mail, too, and I just didn't have time to run back.

STOCKMANN. And you don't give it to me until now!

PETRA. I really didn't have time to run back, Father.

CATHERINE. (*Standing.*) If she didn't have time . . .

STOCKMANN. Let's see it—come on, child . . . (*Slaps* PETRA'S *fanny, takes letter, looks at envelope, recognizes it, crosses* D. R. C.) Yes, indeed.

CATHERINE. Is that the one you've been waiting for?

STOCKMANN. (*Crossing* L. *to study.*) I'll be right back. There wouldn't be a light on in my room, would there? (CATHERINE *takes his glasses out of his pocket as he goes out.*)

CATHERINE. The lamp is on the desk burning away. (*Turns* C.)

STOCKMANN. (*Re-entering* L.) Please excuse me for a moment. (CATHERINE *puts his glasses in his hand as he goes back out* L. *Closes door.* CATHERINE *turns.*)

PETRA. What's that, Mother? (PETRA *crosses slowly to table, fixes drink.*)

CATHERINE. I don't know. The last couple of days he has been asking again and again about the mailman.

BILLING. Probably an out-of-town patient of his. (CATHERINE *sits.*)

PETRA. Poor Father, he's got much too much to do. (*She mixes her drink, comes around sofa.*) This ought to taste good.

HOVSTAD. (*Crossing to* PETRA.) By the way, what happened to that English novel you were going to translate for us?

PETRA. I started to, but I got so busy . . .

HOVSTAD. Oh, have you been teaching evening school again?

PETRA. Two hours a night.

BILLING. Plus the high school every day?

PETRA. Yes, five hours, and every night a pile of lessons to correct . . .

CATHERINE. She never stops going.

HOVSTAD. Maybe that's why I always think of you as kind of breathless, and . . . well, breathless.

PETRA. I love it. I get so wonderfully tired. (PETRA *sits.*)

BILLING. (*To* HORSTER.) She looks tired. (BILLING *crosses* R. *to* R. *chair, all sit.*)

15

MORTEN. (*Crossing to in front of* BILLING.) You must be a wicked woman, Petra. (BILLING *beckons* MORTEN, *who approaches,* EJLIF *follows with nut bowl.*)

PETRA. (*Laughing.*) Wicked?

MORTEN. You work so much. My teacher says that work is a punishment for our sins.

EJLIF. And you believe that?

CATHERINE. Ejlif! Of course he believes his teacher.

BILLING. (*Smiling.*) Don't stop him . . .

HOVSTAD. Don't you like to work, Morten?

MORTEN. Work? No.

HOVSTAD. Then what will you ever amount to in this world?

MORTEN. Me? I'm going to be a Viking.

EJLIF. You can't! You'd have to be a heathen!

MORTEN. So I'll be a heathen.

CATHERINE. (*Rising, crossing* R.; *men rise.*) I think it's getting late, boys . . .

BILLING. I agree with you, Morten; I think . . .

CATHERINE. (*Interrupting* BILLING.) You certainly don't, Mr. Billing.

BILLING. Yes, by God, I do. I'm a real heathen and proud of it. (*Lifts* MORTEN. CATHERINE *tries to stop this violent exercise.*) You'll see, pretty soon we are all going to be heathens.

MORTEN. And then we can do anything we want ——

BILLING. *Right!* You see, Morten . . .

CATHERINE. (*Interrupting.*) Don't you have any homework for tomorrow, boys? Better go in and do it.

EJLIF. Oh, can't we stay in here awhile?

CATHERINE. (*Takes bowl.*) No, neither of you—now run along.

EJLIF. Good night.

MORTEN. Good night. But I don't have any homework . . . (*Boys exit into hall* U. R. HOVSTAD *edges over to* PETRA. CATHERINE *picks up nut bowl, sets it on* R. *table.*)

HOVSTAD. You don't really think it hurts them to listen to such talk, do you? (*Enter* STOCKMANN L.)

CATHERINE. I don't know, but I don't like it. (*As* STOCKMANN *breaks for door* L.) Tom!

STOCKMANN. (*Crossing* C., *open letter in his hand.*) Boys, there is going to be news in this town!

BILLING. News?

CATHERINE. (*Crossing to* STOCKMANN *at* C.) What kind of news? } (*Together.*)

STOCKMANN. Hunh?—A terrific discovery, Catherine.

HOVSTAD. Really?

CATHERINE. That you made? } (*Together.*)

STOCKMANN. (*At* C. *of table.*) That I made. (*Walks back and forth.*) Now let the baboons running this town call me a lunatic! Now they'd better watch out. Oh, how the mighty have fallen! (U. *above* R. *table.*)

PETRA. What is it, Father?

STOCKMANN. Oh, if Peter were only here! Now you'll see how human beings can walk around and make judgments like blind rats.

HOVSTAD. What in the world's happened, Doctor?

STOCKMANN. (*Above table.*) It is the general opinion, isn't it, that our town is a sound and healthy spot?

HOVSTAD. Of course.

CATHERINE. What happened?

STOCKMANN. Even a rather unusually healthy spot —— Oh, God . . . (*Throws his arms up, holding glasses in* L. *hand,* CATHERINE *takes glasses from him, puts them in his pocket.*) a place that can be recommended, not only to all people but sick people.

CATHERINE. But, Tom, what are you ——?

STOCKMANN. And we certainly have recommended it. I myself have written and written about it, in the *People's Messenger,* pamphlets . . .

HOVSTAD. Yes, yes, but, Doctor, what are you trying to say?

STOCKMANN. The miraculous Springs that cost such a fortune to build. The whole Health Institute is a pest hole.

PETRA. Father! The Springs?

CATHERINE. Our Springs? } (*Together.*)

BILLING. That's unbelievable!

STOCKMANN. (*Crossing* R. *to* D. R., *then* L. *to* HORSTER.) You know the filth up in Windmill Valley—that stuff that has such a stinking smell? It comes down from the tannery up there and the same damn poisonous mess comes right out into (*To* HORSTER.) the blessed, miraculous water we're supposed to *cure* people with!

HORSTER. You mean actually where our beaches are?

STOCKMANN. (*At* D. L.) Exactly.

17

HOVSTAD. How are you so sure about this, Doctor?

STOCKMANN. (*Crossing* C. *to* R. *of* HOVSTAD.) I had a suspicion about it a long time ago—last year there were too many sick cases among the visitors; typhoid and gastric disturbances.

CATHERINE. That *did* happen. (*To* BILLING.) I remember Mrs. Svensen's niece . . .

STOCKMANN. (*Crossing to* CATHERINE.) Yes, dear. At the time we thought that the visitors brought the bug, but later this winter I got a new idea and I started investigating the water.

CATHERINE. So that's what you've been working on!

STOCKMANN. I sent samples of the water to the University for an exact chemical analysis.

HOVSTAD. And that's what you have received?

STOCKMANN. (*Showing letter.*) This is it. It proves the existence of infectious organic matter in the water. (*A little pause.* HOVSTAD *is looking at* BILLING.)

CATHERINE. Well, thank God you discovered it in time.

STOCKMANN. I think we can say that, Catherine.

CATHERINE. Isn't it wonderful!

HOVSTAD. And what do you intend to do now, Doctor?

STOCKMANN. Put the thing right, of course.

HOVSTAD. Do you think that can be done?

STOCKMANN. If not, the whole Institute is useless—but there's nothing to worry about—I am quite clear on what has to be done.

CATHERINE. But, Tom, why'd you keep it so secret?

STOCKMANN. What'd you want me to do?—go out and shoot my mouth off before I really knew? No, thanks, I'm not that crazy. (*He walks around, rubbing his hands.*) You don't realize what this means, Catherine—(*Crosses to* BILLING.) the whole water system has got to be changed.

CATHERINE. The *whole* water system?! (*Fades to* L. *above sofa table.*)

STOCKMANN. The whole water system. The intake is too low, it's got to be raised to a much higher spot. The whole construction's got to be ripped out!

PETRA. Well, Dad, at least you can prove they should have listened to you!

STOCKMANN. Ha, she remembers!

CATHERINE. That's right, you did warn them . . .

STOCKMANN. Of course I warned them! When they started the

damned thing I told them not to build it down there. But who am I, a mere scientist to tell politicians where to build a health institute! Well, now they're going to get it both barrels!

BILLING. This is tremendous . . . (*To* HORSTER.) He's a great man!

STOCKMANN. (*Turns.*) It's bigger than tremendous. Wait'll they see this. (*Crosses to* PETRA.) Petra, my report is on my desk . . . (PETRA *sets glass down, runs out* L.) And envelopes, Catherine! (CATHERINE *goes into dining-room,* PETRA *returns with report, gives it to* STOCKMANN.) Gentlemen, this final proof from the University and my report . . . (*Flicks pages.*) five solid, explosive pages . . .

CATHERINE. (*Returns, hands him envelopes.*) Is that big enough?

STOCKMANN. Fine. Right to the Board of Directors! (*Hands report, letter to* CATHERINE.) Will you give this to the maid . . . what's her name again?

CATHERINE. Randine, dear, Randine . . .

STOCKMANN. Tell our darling Randine to wipe her nose and run over to the Mayor right now. (CATHERINE *stands looking at him as though she'd had a little pain.*) What's the matter, dear?

CATHERINE. I don't know . . .

PETRA. What's Uncle Peter going to say to this?

CATHERINE. That's what I'm wondering.

STOCKMANN. What can he say! He ought to be damn glad that such an important fact is brought out before we start an epidemic. Hurry, dear! (CATHERINE *goes into dining-room.*)

HOVSTAD. (*Crossing* R. *from behind sofa between* STOCKMANN *and* PETRA.) I would like to put a brief item about this discovery in the *Messenger.*

STOCKMANN. Yes, now I'd really be grateful for it.

HOVSTAD. Because the public ought to know soon.

STOCKMANN. Right away.

BILLING. By God, you'll be the leading man in this town, Doctor.

STOCKMANN. (*Crossing* BILLING *to* D. R.) Oh, there was nothing to it. Every detective gets a lucky break once in his life. But just the same, I . . .

BILLING. Hovstad, don't you think the town ought to pay Dr. Stockmann some tribute?

STOCKMANN. Oh, no, no . . .

HOVSTAD. Let's all put in a word for . . .

BILLING. (*Crossing* D. R. PETRA *takes drink from sofa table.*) I'll talk to Aslaksen about it. (CATHERINE *enters, crosses* C. HOVSTAD *picks up drink from* R. *table.*)

STOCKMANN. (*Crossing* C.) No, no, fellows, no fooling around. I won't put up with any commotion. Even if the Board of Directors want to give me an increase, I won't take it . . . (*To* CATHERINE.) I just won't take it, Catherine.

CATHERINE. That's right, Tom.

PETRA. (*Lifting glass.*) Skol, Father!

ALL. Skol, Doctor. (*They drink.*)

HORSTER. Doctor, I hope this will bring you great honor and pleasure.

STOCKMANN. Thanks, friends, thanks. There's one blessing above all others: to have earned the respect of one's neighbors is . . . is . . . Catherine, I'm going to dance! (*He grabs* CATHERINE, *starts singing and whirls her around. On second phrase,* PETRA *joins the circle. Boys enter* L., *go* R. *and stand on window seat.* HORSTER, HOVSTAD *and* BILLING *join the dancing circle. All are singing.*)

CATHERINE. (*Seeing boys, screams.*) Children! (*Boys run out* L.)

FAST CURTAIN

ACT I

SCENE 2

SCENE: *The same. The following morning.*

CATHERINE. (*Entering from dining-room with sealed letter, crosses above sofa to* D. L. *door.*) Are you there, Tom?

STOCKMANN. (*Off* L.) I just got in. (*Entering* D. L.; *his coat is buttoned wrong. Closes door.*) What's up?

CATHERINE. (*Giving him letter.*) From Peter. It just came.

STOCKMANN. (*Taking letter.*) Peter! Oh, let's see. (*Opens envelope, reads letter, crosses* C., *holding up letter to catch* R. *sunlight.*) "I am returning herewith the report you submitted . . ."

CATHERINE. (*Following him.*) Well, what does he say? Don't stand there!

STOCKMANN. (*Putting letter in his pocket.*) He just says he'll come around this afternoon.

CATHERINE. (*Buttoning his coat correctly.*) Oh. Well, maybe you ought to try to remember to be home then.

STOCKMANN. Oh, I sure will. I'm through with my morning visits, anyway.

CATHERINE. I'm dying to see how he's going to take it.

STOCKMANN. Why, is there any doubt? He'll probably make it look like he made the discovery, not me.

CATHERINE. But aren't you a little bit afraid of that?

STOCKMANN. Oh, underneath he'll be happy, Catherine. (*Kisses her. One arm is around her.*) It's just that Peter is so damn afraid that somebody else is going to do something good for this town.

CATHERINE. I wish you'd go out of your way and share the honors with him. Couldn't we say that he put you on the right track or something? (KIIL *enters hallway* U. R.)

STOCKMANN. (*Embracing* CATHERINE.) Oh, I don't mind—as long as it makes everybody happy.

KIIL. (*Pokes head into room from hall* U. R., *chuckling.*) Is it really true? (*Crosses* D. R. C.)

CATHERINE. (*Crosses* U. *of* R. C. *table.*) Father! Come on in.

STOCKMANN. (*A step to* KIIL.) Well, good morning!

KIIL. It better be true, or I'm going.

STOCKMANN. What had better be true?

KIIL. (*Crossing to* D. *of* R. *table.*) This crazy story about the water system. Is it true?

CATHERINE. Of course it's true.

STOCKMANN. How did you find out about it?

KIIL. Petra came flying by on her way to school this morning.

STOCKMANN. Oh, she did?

KIIL. Yes. I thought she was trying to make a fool out of me . . .

CATHERINE. Now, Father, why would she do that?

KIIL. Nothing pleases young people more than to make fools out of old people. But this is true, eh?

STOCKMANN. Of course it's true —— (*Seating* KIIL *in* R. C. *chair.* CATHERINE *is above* R. *table.*) Sit down here. It's pretty lucky for the town, eh?

KIIL. (*Fighting his laughter.*) Lucky for the town?!

21

STOCKMANN. I mean that I made the discovery before it was too late.

KIIL. Tom, I never thought you had the imagination to pull your own brother's leg like this.

STOCKMANN. Pull his leg?

CATHERINE. But, Father, he's not . . .

KIIL. How does it go now? Let me get it straight. There's some kind of . . . like cockroaches in the waterpipes . . . ?

STOCKMANN. (*Laughing*.) No, not cockroaches . . .

KIIL. Well, some kind of little animals . . .

CATHERINE. Bacteria, Father . . .

KIIL. Ah, but a whole mess of them, eh?

STOCKMANN. Oh, there'd be millions and millions . . .

KIIL. And nobody can see them but you, is that it?

STOCKMANN. Yes, that's . . . well, of course, anybody with a micro . . . (*Breaks off*.) What are you laughing at?

CATHERINE. (*Smiling at* KIIL.) You don't understand, Father, nobody can actually see bacteria, but that doesn't mean they're not there . . .

KIIL. (*Chuckling*.) Good girl, you stick with him. By God, this is the best thing I ever heard in my life!

STOCKMANN. (*Smiling*.) What do you mean?

KIIL. But tell me, you think you are going to get your brother to actually believe this?

STOCKMANN. Well, we'll see soon enough!

KIIL. You really think he's that crazy?

STOCKMANN. I hope the whole town will be that "crazy," Morten.

KIIL. Ya, they probably are, and it'll serve them right, too—they think they're so much smarter than us old-timers. Your good brother ordered them to bounce me out of the council, so they chased me out like a dog. (*Rising*.) Make jackasses out of all of them, Stockmann.

STOCKMANN. (*Interrupting*.) Yes, but Morten . . .

KIIL. Long-eared, short-tailed jackasses . . . Stockmann, if you can make the Mayor and his elegant friends grab at this bait, I will give a couple hundred crowns to charity, and right now, right on the spot.

STOCKMANN. (*Interrupting*, KIIL *crosses* L. C.) Well, that would be very kind of you, but I'm . . .

KIIL. I haven't got much to play around with, but if you can pull

22

the rug out from under him with this cockroach business, I'll give at least fifty crowns to charity. (HOVSTAD *enters the hall* U. R.) Maybe this'll teach them to put some brains back in City Hall!

HOVSTAD. (*Crossing* D. R.) Good morning! Oh, pardon me ——

STOCKMANN. Come on in.

KIIL. (*Crossing to below table.*) Oh, this one is on it, too?

HOVSTAD. What's that, sir?

STOCKMANN. Of course, he's in on it.

KIIL. Couldn't I have guessed that—and it's going to be in the papers, I suppose. You're sure tying down the corners, aren't you? Well, lay it on thick. I've got to go.

STOCKMANN. Oh, no, stay a while, let me explain it to you!

KIIL. (*Crossing* STOCKMANN *to* L. *of* HOVSTAD.) Oh, I get it, don't worry! Only, you can see them, heh? That's the best idea I've ever heard in my life. (*He goes out* U. R. CATHERINE *then goes off* R. *through dining-room, appears in hall* U. R. *closing portieres tightly.*)

CATHERINE. (*Laughing.*) But, Father, you don't understand about bacteria . . .

STOCKMANN. (*Laughing.*) The old badger doesn't believe a word of it.

HOVSTAD. What does he think you're doing?

STOCKMANN. Making an idiot out of my brother, imagine that?

HOVSTAD. (*Crossing* STOCKMANN *to* C.) You got a few minutes?

STOCKMANN. Sure, as long as you like.

HOVSTAD. Have you heard from the Mayor?

STOCKMANN. Only that he's coming over later.

HOVSTAD. I've been thinking about this since last night . . . (*Crosses to* STOCKMANN.)

STOCKMANN. Don't say?

HOVSTAD. For you as a medical man, a scientist, this is a really rare opportunity. But I've been wondering if you realize that it ties in with a lot of other things.

STOCKMANN. How do you mean? Sit down —— (*They sit,* STOCKMANN *in* R. *chair,* HOVSTAD *in* R. C. *chair.*) What are you driving at?

HOVSTAD. You said last night that the water comes from impurities in the ground ——

STOCKMANN. It comes from the poisonous dump in Windmill Valley.

HOVSTAD. Doctor, I think it comes from an entirely different dump —the same dump that is poisoning and polluting our whole social life in this town.

STOCKMANN. For God's sake, Hovstad, what are you babbling about?

HOVSTAD. Everything that matters in this town has fallen into the hands of a few bureaucrats.

STOCKMANN. Well, they're not all bureaucrats ——

HOVSTAD. They're all rich—all with old reputable names and they've got everything in the palm of their hands.

STOCKMANN. Yes, but they happen to have ability and knowledge.

HOVSTAD. Did they show ability and knowledge when they built the water system where they did?

STOCKMANN. No, of course not, but that happened to be a blunder and we'll clear it up now.

HOVSTAD. You really imagine it's going to be as easy as all that?

STOCKMANN. Easy or not easy, it's got to be done.

HOVSTAD. Doctor, I've made up my mind to give this whole scandal very special treatment.

STOCKMANN. Now wait—you can't call it a scandal yet.

HOVSTAD. Doctor, when I took over the *People's Messenger*, I swore I'd blow that smug cabal of old, stubborn, self-satisfied fogies to bits. This is the story that can do it.

STOCKMANN. But I still think we owe them a deep debt of gratitude for building the Springs.

HOVSTAD. The Mayor being your brother, I wouldn't ordinarily want to touch it, but I know you'd never let that kind of thing obstruct the truth.

STOCKMANN. Of course not, but . . .

HOVSTAD. I want you to understand me. I don't have to tell you I come from a simple family. I know in my bones what the underdog needs—he's got to have a say in the government of society— that's what brings out ability, intelligence, and self-respect in people.

STOCKMANN. I understand that, but . . .

HOVSTAD. I think a newspaper man who turns down any chance to give the underdog a lift is taking on a responsibility that I don't want. (*Rises, paces* C. *and back to table.*) I know perfectly well that in fancy circles they call it agitation, and they can call it anything they like if it makes them happy—but I have my own conscience!

STOCKMANN. (*Interrupting.*) I agree with you, Hovstad . . . (ASLAKSEN *knocks, then enters* U. R.) but this is just the water supply and . . . (STOCKMANN *rises, crosses* R. *and* U.) Damn it, come in.

ASLAKSEN. (*Entering from* U. R.) I beg your pardon, Doctor, if I intrude . . . (STOCKMANN *takes him by* R. *arm and brings him* D. C.)

HOVSTAD. (*Crossing* D. R.) Are you looking for me, Aslaksen?

ASLAKSEN. No, I didn't know you were here. I want to see the Doctor.

STOCKMANN. What can I do for you?

ASLAKSEN. Is it true, Doctor, what I hear from Mr. Billing that you intend to campaign for a better water system?

STOCKMANN. (*Offers chair.*) Yes, for the Institute—but it's not a campaign.

ASLAKSEN. I just wanted to call and tell you that we are behind you one hundred percent.

HOVSTAD. (*To* STOCKMANN.) There, you see . . .

STOCKMANN. Mr. Aslaksen, I thank you with all my heart, but, you see . . .

ASLAKSEN. We can be important, Doctor. When the little business man wants to push something through, he turns out to be the majority, you know, and it's always good to have the majority on your side.

STOCKMANN. That's certainly true, but I don't understand what this is all about. It seems to me it's a simple, straightforward business. The water . . .

ASLAKSEN. Of course, we intend to behave with moderation, Doctor. I always try to be a moderate and careful man.

STOCKMANN. You are known for that, Mr. Aslaksen, but . . .

ASLAKSEN. Kirsten Springs are becoming a gold mine for this town. Especially for the little businessmen, and that's why, in my capacity as Chairman of the Property Owners' Association . . .

STOCKMANN. Yes . . .

ASLAKSEN. And furthermore, as a representative of the Temperance Society—you probably know, Doctor, that I am active for prohibition.

STOCKMANN. So I've heard.

25

ASLAKSEN. As a result, I come into contact with all kinds of people, and since I'm known to be a law-abiding and solid citizen, I have a certain influence in this town—(*Advancing a little to* HOVSTAD.) you might even call it a little power.

STOCKMANN. I know that very well, Mr. Aslaksen.

ASLAKSEN. That's why you can see that it would be practically nothing for me to arrange a demonstration.

STOCKMANN. Demonstration? What are you going to demonstrate about?

ASLAKSEN. The citizens of the town complimenting you for bringing this important matter to everybody's attention. Obviously it would have to be done with the utmost moderation so as not to hurt the authorities . . .

HOVSTAD. This could knock the big-bellies right into the garbage can!

ASLAKSEN. (*Crossing to* HOVSTAD.) No indiscretion or extreme aggressiveness toward the authorities, Mr. Hovstad! (HOVSTAD *crosses to window seat* R., *sits, takes notes.*) I don't want any wild-eyed radicalism on this thing. (ASLAKSEN *to* STOCKMANN.) I've had enough of that in my time, and no good ever comes of it, but for a good solid citizen to express his calm, frank and free opinion is something nobody can deny.

STOCKMANN. (*Shaking his hand.*) My dear Aslaksen, I can't tell you how it heartens me to hear this kind of support. I'm happy— I really am—I'm happy. Listen! Wouldn't you like a glass of sherry?

ASLAKSEN. I am a member of the Temperance Society, I ——

STOCKMANN. Well, how about a glass of beer?

ASLAKSEN. I don't think I can go quite that far, Doctor. Well, good day, and I want you to remember that the little man is behind you like a wall. You have the solid majority on your side, because when the little man takes over . . .

STOCKMANN. (*Takes his arm, crosses* ASLAKSEN *in front and starts out* U. R.) Thanks for that, Mr. Aslaksen—and good day.

ASLAKSEN. Are you going to the printing shop, Mr. Hovstad?

HOVSTAD. I just have a thing or two to attend to here.

ASLAKSEN. Very well. (*He leaves* U. R.; STOCKMANN *follows him into hall, then returns* D. R.)

HOVSTAD. (*Rising, puts notes in pocket, crosses* C.) Well, what do you say to a little hypodermic for these fence-sitting deadheads?

Everybody's afraid—afraid—they know perfectly well what's right, but they're afraid.

STOCKMANN. Why? I think that Aslaksen is a very sincere man.

HOVSTAD. Isn't it time we pumped some guts into these well-intentioned men of good-will? Under all their liberal talk, they still idolize authority and that's got to be rooted out of this town. This blunder of the water system has to be made clear to every voter. Let me print your report.

STOCKMANN. (*Turning away a little.*) Not until I talk to my brother.

HOVSTAD. I'll write an editorial in the meantime, and if the Mayor won't go along with us ——

STOCKMANN. I don't see how you can imagine such a thing!

HOVSTAD. Believe me, Doctor, it's entirely possible . . .

STOCKMANN. Listen. I promise you: he will go along and then you can print my report, every word of it.

HOVSTAD. On your word of honor?

STOCKMANN. (*Giving him manuscript.*) Here it is, take it. It can't do any harm for you to read it. Return it to me later.

HOVSTAD. (*Takes manuscript, puts it in his pocket, starts out* U. R.) Good day, Doctor.

STOCKMANN. Good day. You will see it's going to be easier than you think.

HOVSTAD. (*Stops.*) I hope so, Doctor, sincerely. Let me know as soon as you hear from His Honor. (*Goes out* U. R.)

STOCKMANN. (*Crosses and looks in dining-room.*) Catherine! Oh, you're home already, Petra.

PETRA. (*Entering dining-room from* L. *with glass of milk.*) I just got back from school. (*Comes into room, kisses* STOCKMANN, *crosses to stove to warm back.* CATHERINE *enters from dining-room.*)

CATHERINE. Hasn't he been here yet?

STOCKMANN. Peter? No, but I just had a long chat with Hovstad. (*Leading* CATHERINE D. C.) He's really fascinated with my discovery and, you know, it has more implications than I thought at first. Do you know what I have backing me up?

CATHERINE. What, in heaven's name, have you got backing you up?

STOCKMANN. The solid majority.

CATHERINE. Is that good? (PETRA *crosses* D., *sits on* D. *arm of sofa.*)

STOCKMANN. Good? It's wonderful. You can't imagine the feeling, Catherine, to know that your own town feels like a brother to you. I haven't felt so at home in this town since I was a boy. (*Doorbell.*)

CATHERINE. That's the front door. (*She crosses* U. *around table to hall* U. R.; *lets* PETER *in.*)

STOCKMANN. Oh, it's Peter, then. Come in. (PETER *enters from hall* U. R. PETRA *rises.*)

PETER. (*Crossing* D. R.) Good morning!

CATHERINE. Good morning.

STOCKMANN. It's nice to see you, Peter.

CATHERINE. How are you today?

PETER. Well, so-so . . . (CATHERINE *crosses* U. *to* R. *of* PETRA; PETER *to* STOCKMANN.) I received your thesis about the condition of the Springs yesterday. (*Crosses* L., *puts hat on* R. C. *table, crosses* C., *turns to face* STOCKMANN.)

STOCKMANN. I got your note. Did you read it?

PETER. I read it.

STOCKMANN. Well, what do you have to say? (PETER *clears his throat, glances aside.*)

CATHERINE. Come on, Petra. (*She and* PETRA *exit* L., *closing door.*)

PETER. (*After a moment.*) Thomas, was it really necessary to go into this investigation behind my back?

STOCKMANN. Yes, until I was convinced myself, there was no point in . . .

PETER. And now you are convinced?

STOCKMANN. Well, certainly—aren't you, too, Peter? (*Pause.*) The University chemists corroborated . . .

PETER. You intend to present this document to the Board of Directors, officially, as the Medical Officer of the Springs?

STOCKMANN. Of course, something's got to be done, and quick.

PETER. You always use such strong expressions, Thomas. (*Sits* C. *of sofa.*) Among other things, in your report, you say that we *guarantee* our guests and visitors a permanent case of poisoning.

STOCKMANN. Yes, but, Peter, how can you describe it any other way? Imagine! Poisoned internally and externally!

PETER. So you merrily conclude that we must build a waste disposal plant—and reconstruct a brand new water system from the bottom up?

STOCKMANN. (*Taking* R. C. *chair, moves it* C. *as though to sit.*) Well, do you know some other way out? I don't.

PETER. I took a little walk over to the City Engineer this morning and in the course of conversation I sort of jokingly mentioned these changes—as something we might consider for the future, you know.

STOCKMANN. The future won't be soon enough, Peter.

PETER. The Engineer kind of smiled at my extravagance and gave me a few facts. I don't suppose you've taken the trouble to consider what your proposed changes would cost?

STOCKMANN. No, I never thought of that . . .

PETER. Naturally. Your little project would come to at least three hundred thousand crowns.

STOCKMANN. (*Sitting.*) That expensive?

PETER. Oh, don't look so upset—it's only money. The worst thing is that it would take some two years.

STOCKMANN. Two years?

PETER. At the least, and what do you propose we do about the Springs in the meantime—shut them up, no doubt! Because we'd have to, you know. As soon as the rumor gets around that the water is dangerous, we won't have a visitor left. And that's the picture, Thomas—you have it in your power to literally ruin your own town.

STOCKMANN. (*Rises.*) Now look, Peter! I don't want to ruin anything.

PETER. Thomas, your report has not convinced me that the conditions are as dangerous as you try to make them.

STOCKMANN. Now, listen, they are even worse than the report makes them out to be. Remember, summer is coming, and the warm weather.

PETER. I think you're exaggerating. A capable physician ought to know what precautions to take.

STOCKMANN. And then what?

PETER. The existing water supplies for the Springs are a fact, Thomas, and they've got to be treated as a fact. If you are reasonable and act with discretion, the Directors of the Institute will be inclined to take under consideration any means to reasonably and without financial sacrifices make possible improvements.

29

STOCKMANN. Dear God, do you think for one minute that I would ever agree to such trickery?

PETER. Trickery?

STOCKMANN. Yes, a trick, a fraud, a lie, a treachery—a downright crime against the public and against the whole community.

PETER. I said before that I'm not convinced that there is any actual danger.

STOCKMANN. Oh, you aren't? Anything else is impossible! My report is an absolute fact. (*Turns, violently replaces chair, steps* D.) The only trouble is that you and your administration were the ones who insisted that the water supply be built where it is, and now you're afraid to admit the blunder you committed. Damn it! Don't you think I can see through it all?

PETER. (*Rises, crosses* D. C.) All right, let's suppose that is true. Maybe I do care a little about my reputation. I still say I do it for the good of the town; without moral authority there can be no government. *And that is why, Thomas, it is my duty to prevent your report from reaching the Board.* Some time later I will bring up the matter for discussion. In the meantime, not a single word is to reach the public.

STOCKMANN. Oh, my dear Peter, do you imagine you can prevent that!

PETER. It will be prevented.

STOCKMANN. It can't be. There are too many people who already know about it.

PETER. Who? (*Angered.*) It can't possibly be those people from the *Daily Messenger* who . . .

STOCKMANN. Exactly. The liberal, free and independent press will stand up and do its duty!

PETER. You are an unbelievably irresponsible man, Thomas. Can't you imagine what consequences that is going to have for you?

STOCKMANN. For me?

PETER. Yes, for you and your family.

STOCKMANN. (*Turning away.*) What the hell are you saying now?

PETER. I believe I have the right to think of myself as a helpful brother, Thomas.

STOCKMANN. You have been and I thank you deeply for it.

PETER. Don't mention it. I often couldn't help myself. I had hoped that by improving your finances I would be able to keep you from running *completely* hog-wild.

30

STOCKMANN. You mean it was only for your own sake?

PETER. Partly yes. What do you imagine people think of an official whose closest relatives get themselves into trouble time and time again?

STOCKMANN. And that's what I've done?

PETER. You do it without knowing it—you're like a man with an automatic brain—as soon as an idea breaks into your head, no matter how idiotic it may be—you get up like a sleep-walker and start writing a pamphlet.

STOCKMANN. (*Steps to* PETER.) Peter, don't you think it's a citizen's duty to share a new idea with the public?

PETER. (*Crossing* D. L. C.) The public doesn't need new ideas—the public is much better off with old ideas.

STOCKMANN. You're not even embarrassed to say that?

PETER. (*Crossing to* STOCKMANN.) Now look, I am going to lay this out once and for all. You're always barking about authority. If a man gives you an order, he's persecuting you. Nothing is important enough to respect, once you decide to revolt against your superiors. All right, then, I give up. I'm not going to try to change you any more. I told you the stakes you are playing for here, and now I'm going to give you an order and I warn you, you'd better obey it if you value your career.

STOCKMANN. What kind of an order?

PETER. You are going to deny these rumors officially.

STOCKMANN. How?

PETER. You simply say that you went into the examination of the water more thoroughly and you find that you overestimated the danger.

STOCKMANN. I see!

PETER. And that you have complete confidence that whatever improvements are needed, the management will certainly take care of them.

STOCKMANN. My convictions come from the conditions of the water. My convictions will change when the water changes, and for no other reason.

PETER. What are you talking about convictions? You're an official, you keep your convictions to yourself!

STOCKMANN. To myself?!

PETER. As an official, I said. God knows as a private person that is something else, but as a subordinate employee of the Institute, you have no right to express any convictions or personal opinions about anything connected with policy!

STOCKMANN. Now you listen to me! I am a doctor and a scientist!!

PETER. What's this got to do with science?

STOCKMANN. And I have the right to express my opinion on anything in the world!

PETER. Not about the Institute—that I forbid.

STOCKMANN. You forbid!

PETER. I forbid you as your superior, and when I give orders you obey.

STOCKMANN. (*Turning away from* PETER.) Peter, if you weren't my brother . . .

PETRA. (*Throws* L. *door open, flies in,* CATHERINE *tries to restrain her,* PETRA *crosses to* L. *of* PETER.) Father! You aren't going to stand for this!

CATHERINE. (*Following* PETRA.) Petra, Petra . . .

PETER. What have you two been doing, eavesdropping?

CATHERINE. You were talking so loud we couldn't help . . .

PETRA. (*Interrupting.*) Yes, I was eavesdropping.

PETER. (*Crossing below* STOCKMANN *to his* R.) That makes me very happy.

STOCKMANN. (*Moving* L.) You said something to me about forbidding ——

PETER. You forced me to.

STOCKMANN. So, you want me to spit in my own face officially, is that it?

PETER. Why must you always be so colorful?

STOCKMANN. And if I don't obey?

PETER. Then we will publish our own statement, to calm the public.

STOCKMANN. Good enough! And I will write against you. I will stick to what I said, and I will prove that I am right and that you are wrong, and what will you do then?

PETER. Then I simply won't be able to prevent your dismissal.

STOCKMANN. (*Steps back.*) What!   } (*Together.*)
PETRA. (*Steps to* C.) Father!

PETER. Dismissed from the Institute is what I said. If you want to make war on Kirsten Springs, you have no right to be on the Board of Directors.

STOCKMANN. You'd dare to do that?

PETER. Oh, no, you're the daring man.

PETRA. (*Crossing to* PETER, *below* STOCKMANN, *who crosses* D. C., *head in hands.*) Uncle, this is a rotten way to treat a man like Father.

CATHERINE. (*Crossing below* STOCKMANN, *to* PETRA.) Will you be quiet, Petra.

PETER. So young and you've got opinions already—but that's natural. (*To* CATHERINE.) Catherine, dear, you're probably the only sane person in this house. Knock some sense into his head, will you? Make him realize what he's driving his whole family into.

STOCKMANN. (*Crossing below to* PETER, *puts family behind him.*) My family concerns nobody but myself.

PETER. His family and his own town!

STOCKMANN. I'm going to show you who loves his town. The people are going to get the full stink of this corruption, Peter, and then we will see who loves his town.

PETER. You love your town when you blindly, spitefully, stubbornly go ahead trying to cut off our most important industry?

STOCKMANN. That source is poisoned, man. We are getting fat by peddling filth and corruption to innocent people!

PETER. I think this has gone beyond opinions and convictions, Thomas. A man who can throw that kind of insinuation around is nothing but a traitor to society!

STOCKMANN. (*Striving to control self.*) How dare you to . . . ?

CATHERINE. (*Running in front of* STOCKMANN; PETRA *pulls* STOCKMANN *back.*) Tom!

PETRA. (*Grabbing* STOCKMANN'S *arm.*) Be careful, Father!

PETER. (*Taking hat, starting out* U. R., *with dignity.*) I won't expose myself to violence. You have been warned. Consider what you owe yourself and your family. Good day! (*He exits* U. R., *leaving front door open.*)

STOCKMANN. (*Pacing* D. R., *then back to* D. L.) He's insulted! He's insulted!

CATHERINE. (*Crossing* U. C., D. R., *then* L.) It's shameful, Thomas.

PETRA. (*Crossing* U. L. C., *to stove, then* R. *to look after* PETER, *back to* C. *at* R. *of* CATHERINE.) Oh, I would love to give him a piece of my mind.

STOCKMANN. (*Still pacing.*) It was my own fault—I should have shown my teeth right from the beginning. He called me a traitor to society. Me! Damn it all, that is not going to stick.

CATHERINE. Please, think; he's got all the power on his side.

STOCKMANN. Yes, but I have the truth on mine.

CATHERINE. Without power, what good is the truth? (*All turn and look at her.*)

STOCKMANN. (*Crosses to* CATHERINE.) That's ridiculous, Catherine. I have the liberal press with me and the majority, the solid majority. If that isn't power, what is?

CATHERINE. But for Heaven's sake, Tom, you aren't going to . . . ?

STOCKMANN. What am I not going to do ——?

CATHERINE. You aren't going to fight it out in public with your brother!

STOCKMANN. What the hell else do you want me to do?

CATHERINE. But it won't do you any earthly good—if they won't do it, they won't. All you'll get out of it is a notice that you're fired.

STOCKMANN. I am going to do my duty, Catherine. Me, the man he calls a traitor to society!

CATHERINE. And how about your duty to your family—the people you're supposed to provide for?

PETRA. Don't always think of us first, Mother.

CATHERINE. You can talk—if worst comes to worst, you can manage for yourself, but what about the boys, Tom, and you and me?

STOCKMANN. What about you? You want me to be the miserable animal who'd crawl up the boots of that damn gang? Will you be happy if I can't face *myself* the rest of my life?

CATHERINE. Tom, Tom, there's so much injustice in the world— you've simply got to learn to live with it. If you go on this way, God help us, we'll have no money again. Is it so long since the North that you have forgotten what it was to live like we lived? (MORTEN *and* EJLIF *enter hall* U. R. *with school-books.* CATHERINE *sees them.*) Haven't we had enough of that for one lifetime? What will happen to them? We've got nothing if you are fired . . . ! (*The boys have entered heartily, they cross* D. R., *then to* R. *of family.*)

STOCKMANN. (*After seeing boys enter.*) Stop it! (*To boys, who are frightened by this scene.*) Well, boys, did you learn anything in school today?

24

MORTEN. We learned what an insect is . . .

STOCKMANN. You don't say!

MORTEN. (*To* STOCKMANN.) What happened here? (*Crosses to* L. *of* STOCKMANN; *to* CATHERINE.) Why is everybody . . . ?

STOCKMANN. (*Calming boys.*) Nothing, nothing! You know what I'm going to do, boys? From now on, I'm going to *teach you what a man is!* (CATHERINE *cries.*)

MEDIUM FAST CURTAIN

ACT II

Scene 1

The Editorial Office of " The People's Daily Messenger."
The front door of the office is D. R. U. R. *is* BILLING'S
desk and chair. A wastebasket is downstage of desk. A
large table, covered with newspapers, measures, etc., is
C. *with two chairs,* U. *and* R. *A door leading to printing*
shop is U. L. D. L. *is a door to a small room. The room*
is dingy and cheerless, the furniture shabby, the chairs
dirty.
BILLING *is sitting at his desk* U. R., *reading* STOCKMANN'S
manuscript. After a moment, HOVSTAD *enters* U. L.,
carrying a ruler. BILLING *looks up.*

BILLING. Doctor not come yet?
HOVSTAD. (*Crossing to* BILLING, *looks over his shoulder.*) No, not
yet. You finish it. (BILLING *holds up a hand to signal " just a mo-*
ment." He reads on. After a moment he closes manuscript with
a bang, glances up at HOVSTAD *with some trepidation, then looks*
off. HOVSTAD, *looking at* BILLING, *walks a few steps to* C. D. *table,*
sets ruler down, puts on coat.) Well? What do you think of it?
BILLING. (*As though with some hesitation.*) It's devastating. The
Doctor is a brilliant man. I swear I myself never really under-
stood how incompetent those fat fellows are, on top. (*Holding*
manuscript, rises, waves it a little.) I hear the rumble of revolu-
tion in this.
HOVSTAD. (*Glances at* U. L. *door, takes* BILLING D. R. C.) Sssh!
Aslaksen's inside.
BILLING. Aslaksen's a coward. With all that moderation talk, all
he's saying is, he's yellow. You're going to print this, aren't you?
HOVSTAD. Sure, I'm just waiting for the Doctor to give the word.
And if his brother hasn't given in, we put it on the press anyway.
BILLING. Yes, but if the Mayor is against this it's going to get
pretty rough. You know that, don't you?
HOVSTAD. Just let him try to block that reconstruction—the little

businessmen and the whole town'll be screaming for his head. Aslaksen'll see to that.

BILLING. (*Holding up manuscript.*) But the stockholders'll have to lay out a fortune of money if this goes through.

HOVSTAD. My boy, I think it's going to bust them! And when the Springs go busted, the people are finally going to understand the level of genius that's been running this town. Those five sheets of paper are going to put in a liberal administration once and for all.

BILLING. It's a revolution. You know that? (*With hope and fear.*) I mean it, we're on the edge of a real revolution! (STOCKMANN *enters* D. R., *takes manuscript from* BILLING, *holds it out to* HOVSTAD, *but doesn't give it to him.*)

STOCKMANN. Put it on the press!

BILLING. (*Over* STOCKMANN'S *lines, crossing* U. L., *calling into shop.*) Mr. Aslaksen! The Doctor's here! (*Crosses* D. *to* L. C.)

HOVSTAD. Wonderful! What'd the Mayor say?

STOCKMANN. The Mayor has declared war, so war is what it's going to be. (*Crosses back in front of* HOVSTAD.) And this is only the beginning! You know what he tried to do? . . . He actually tried to blackmail me! He's got the nerve to tell me that I'm not allowed to speak my mind without his permission. Imagine the shameless effrontery!

HOVSTAD. He actually said it right out!?

STOCKMANN. Right to my face! The trouble with me was I kept giving them credit for being our kind of people, but they're *dictators!* (ASLAKSEN *enters* U. L., *crosses* U. *to* R. *of* STOCKMANN.) They're people who'll try to hold power even if they have to poison the town to do it!

ASLAKSEN. Now take it easy, Doctor, you . . . mustn't always be throwing accusations. I'm with you, you understand, but—moderation.

STOCKMANN. (*Cutting him off.*) What'd you think of the article, Hovstad?

HOVSTAD. It's a masterpiece. In one blow you've managed to prove beyond any doubt what kind of men are running us.

ASLAKSEN. May we print it now, then?

STOCKMANN. I should say *so!*

HOVSTAD. (*Reaching for manuscript.*) We'll have it ready for tomorrow's paper.

STOCKMANN. And, listen, Mr. Aslaksen, do me a favor, will you?

You run a fine paper, but supervise the printing personally, heh? I'd hate to see the weather report stuck into the middle of my article.

ASLAKSEN. (*Laughs.*) Don't worry, there won't be a mistake this time!

STOCKMANN. Make it perfect, heh? Like you were printing money. You can't imagine how I'm dying to see it in print. After all the lies in the papers, the half lies, the quarter lies—to finally see the absolute, unvarnished truth about something important . . . ! And this is only the beginning. We'll go on to other subjects, and blow up every lie we live by! What do you say, Aslaksen?

ASLAKSEN. (*Nods in agreement, but.*) Just remember . . .

BILLING and HOVSTAD. (*Together with* ASLAKSEN.) " Moderation! " (BILLING *and* HOVSTAD *are greatly amused.*)

ASLAKSEN. (*To* BILLING *and* HOVSTAD.) I don't see what's so funny about that!

BILLING. (*Crossing above table to* STOCKMANN, *enthralled.* HOVSTAD *gives* L.) Doctor Stockmann . . . I feel as though I were standing in some historic painting. Goddammit, this is a historic day! Some day this scene'll be in a museum. Entitled, " The Day the Truth Was Born." (*All are embarrassed by this.* ASLAKSEN *and* HOVSTAD *look away.*)

STOCKMANN. (*Suddenly.*) Oh! I've got a patient half-bandaged down the road. (*Crosses to door* D. R., *returns and exclaims " Oh," gives* BILLING *manuscript.* BILLING *follows, takes manuscript from* STOCKMANN, *who exits* D. R.)

HOVSTAD. (*Moving to* ASLAKSEN.) I hope you realize how useful he could be to us.

ASLAKSEN. (*Crossing* HOVSTAD *to* D. L. C.) I don't like that business about " this is only the beginning." Let him stick to the Springs.

BILLING. (*Crossing* HOVSTAD *to* ASLAKSEN. HOVSTAD *takes manuscript from* BILLING, *studies it.*) What makes you so scared all the time?

ASLAKSEN. I have to live here. It'd be different if he were attacking the national Government or something, but if he thinks I'm going to start going after the whole town administration . . .

BILLING. What's the difference, bad is bad!

ASLAKSEN. Yes, but there is a difference. You attack the national Government, what's going to happen? Nothing. They go right on.

But a town administration—they're liable to be overthrown or something! I represent the small property owners in this town . . .

BILLING. Ha! It's always the same. Give a man a little property and the truth can go to hell!

ASLAKSEN. Mr. Billing, I'm older than you are; I've seen fire-eaters before. (*Points to* BILLING'S *desk.*) You know who used to work at your desk before you? Councilman Stensford—*Councilman!*

BILLING. Just because I work at a renegade's desk, does that mean . . . ?

ASLAKSEN. You're a politician; a politician never knows where he's going to end up. And, besides, you applied for a job as secretary to the Magistrate, didn't you?

HOVSTAD. Billing!

BILLING. (*To* HOVSTAD.) Well, why not? If I get it I'll have a chance to put across some good things —— (*Turns back to* ASLAKSEN.) I could put plenty of big boys on the spot with a job like that!

ASLAKSEN. All right, I'm just saying . . . People change. Just remember, when you call me a coward—I may not have made the hot speeches, but I never went back on my beliefs, either. Unlike some of the big radicals around here, I didn't change. Of course, I *am* a little more moderate . . .

HOVSTAD. Oh, God!

ASLAKSEN. (*Glaring at* HOVSTAD.) I don't see what's so funny about that! (*He goes out* D. L.)

BILLING. (*After watching him off.*) If we could get rid of him, we . . .

HOVSTAD. Take it easy, he pays the printing bill, he's not that bad. (*Crosses to* BILLING, *with manuscript.*) I'll get the printer on this . . . (*Starts out to* U. L. *door.*)

BILLING. Say, Hovstad, how about asking Stockmann to back us? Then we could really put out a paper!

HOVSTAD. What would he do for money?

BILLING. His father-in-law.

HOVSTAD. Kiil? Since when has he got money?

BILLING. I think he's loaded with it.

HOVSTAD. No! Really, as long as I've known him, he's worn the same overcoat, the same suit . . .

BILLING. Yeah, and the same ring on his right hand. You ever get a look at that boulder? (*Points to his finger.*)

HOVSTAD. No, I never . . .

BILLING. All year he wears the diamond inside. But on New Year's Eve, he turns it around. Figure it out, when a man has no visible means of support, what's he living on?—Money, right? Now, my idea is . . . (PETRA *enters* D. R., *carrying a book.*)

PETRA. Hello.

HOVSTAD. (*Stepping down a little.*) Well, fancy seeing you here! Sit down, what . . . ?

PETRA. (*Tossing book on* BILLING'S *desk with a certain peeve.*) I want to ask you something.

BILLING. (*Crossing* U. *to desk.*) What's that?

PETRA. That English novel you wanted translated.

HOVSTAD. Aren't you going to do it?

PETRA. (*Crossing to* HOVSTAD *at* C.) I don't get this?

HOVSTAD. You don't get what?

PETRA. This book is absolutely against everything you people believe.

HOVSTAD. Oh, it isn't that bad . . . (*Looks at* BILLING; *neither has read it.*)

PETRA. But, Mr. Hovstad, it says if you're good there's a supernatural force that'll fix it so you end up happy. And if you're bad, you'll be punished. Since when does the world work that way?

HOVSTAD. Yeah, but, Petra, this is a newspaper; people like to read that kind of thing. They buy the paper for that and then we slip in our political stuff. A newspaper can't buck the public . . .

PETRA. You don't say! (*She starts to go out* D. R. HOVSTAD *hurries to her, grabs her arm at door, holds her.*)

HOVSTAD. Now, wait a minute. I don't want you to go feeling that way. (*Holds out manuscript to* BILLING.) Here, take this to the printer, will you?

BILLING. (*Taking it.*) Sure. (*He exits* U. L.)

HOVSTAD. (*Leading her back to* C.) I just want you to understand something: I never even read that book. It was Billing's idea.

PETRA. I thought he was a radical.

HOVSTAD. He is. But he's also a . . .

PETRA. A newspaper man.

40

HOVSTAD. Well, that, too. But I was going to say that Billing is trying to get the job as secretary to the Magistrate.

PETRA. What?

HOVSTAD. People are people, Miss Stockmann.

PETRA. But, the Magistrate! He's been fighting everything progressive in this town for thirty years.

HOVSTAD. Let's not argue about it, I just didn't want you to go out of here with a wrong idea of me. I guess you know that I . . . happen to admire women like you. I've never had a chance to tell you, but I . . . well, I want you to know it. Do you mind? (*He smiles.*)

PETRA. No, I don't mind, but reading that book upset me. I really don't understand. . . . Will you tell me why you're supporting my father?

HOVSTAD. What's the mystery? It's a matter of principle.

PETRA. But a paper that'll print a book like that has no principle.

HOVSTAD. Why do you jump to such extremes! You're just like . . .

PETRA. Like what?

HOVSTAD. I simply meant that . . .

PETRA. Like my father, you meant. You really have no use for him, do you?

HOVSTAD. (*Chiding a little, takes her arms, guides her back.*) Now wait a minute!

PETRA. What's behind this? Are you just trying to hold my hand or something?

HOVSTAD. I happen to agree with your father, and that's why I'm printing his stuff! Nothing would please me more than to hold your hand, Miss Stockmann, but I assure you this . . .

PETRA. You're trying to put something over, I think. Why are you in this?

HOVSTAD. Who are you accusing? Billing gave you that book, not me!

PETRA. But you don't mind printing it, do you? What're you trying to do with my father?—you have no principles, what are you up to here?! (ASLAKSEN, *manuscript in his hand, hurriedly enters from* D. L. *door, looking off. He closes door.*)

ASLAKSEN. My God! Hovstad! (*Sees* PETRA, *stops.* PETRA, *frightened, jumps to* R. *of* HOVSTAD.) Miss Stockmann!

PETRA. I don't think I've been so frightened in my life. (*She goes out* D. R. HOVSTAD *starts after her.*)

41

HOVSTAD. (*Following her.*) Please, you mustn't think I . . .

ASLAKSEN. (*As* HOVSTAD *starts to move, following and stopping him.*) Where are you going? The Mayor's out there.

HOVSTAD. The Mayor!

ASLAKSEN. He wants to speak to you. He came in the back door. He doesn't want to be seen.

HOVSTAD. (*Crossing to* D. L. *door.*) What does he want?

ASLAKSEN. I'll watch for anyone coming in here.

HOVSTAD. (*Opening* D. L. *door.*) Come in, Your Honor!

PETER. (*Entering* D. L. *and looking the place over.*) Thank you. (*He crosses* HOVSTAD. HOVSTAD *carefully closes* D. L. *door.*) It's clean! I always imagined this place would look dirty. But it's clean. (*Sets hat on* BILLING'S *desk.*) Very nice, Mr. Aslaksen.

ASLAKSEN. Not at all, Your Honor. I mean to say I always . . .

HOVSTAD. (*Crossing to* L. *of table.*) What can I do for you, Your Honor? (*Offers him* U. L. *chair, but* PETER *is sitting in* L. C. *chair.*) Sit down?

PETER. I had a very annoying thing happen today, Mr. Hovstad.

HOVSTAD. That so?

PETER. It seems my brother has written some sort of . . . memorandum. About the Springs.

HOVSTAD. You don't say! (ASLAKSEN *starts to fade to* U. L. *door.*)

PETER. (*Looking at* HOVSTAD *now.*) Ah . . . he mentioned it . . . to you?

HOVSTAD. Ah . . . yes. I think he said something about it.

PETER. (*Points to manuscript, stopping* ASLAKSEN *at* U. L. *door.*) That's it, isn't it?

ASLAKSEN. This? (*Crosses to* R. *of* PETER.) I don't know, I haven't had a chance to look at it, the printer just handed it to me . . .

HOVSTAD. (*Crossing* U. *a little, speaking behind* PETER.) Isn't that the thing the printer wanted the spelling checked?

ASLAKSEN. That's it, it's only a question of spelling. I'll be right back . . .

PETER. I'm very good at spelling. (*Holds out his hand.*) Maybe I can help you?

HOVSTAD. No, Your Honor, there's some Latin in it . . . you wouldn't know Latin, would you?

PETER. Oh, yes. I used to help my brother with his Latin all the time. Let me have it. (ASLAKSEN *gives him manuscript.* PETER *looks at title on first page, then glances up at* HOVSTAD, *who avoids his eyes.*) You're going to print this?

HOVSTAD. I can't very well refuse a signed article. A signed article is the author's responsibility.

PETER. (*Holding up manuscript.*) Mr. Aslaksen, you're going to allow this?

ASLAKSEN. I'm the publisher, not the editor, Your Honor. My policy is, freedom for the editor.

PETER. You have a point; I can see that.

ASLAKSEN. (*Reaching for manuscript.*) So if you don't mind . . .

PETER. Not at all. (*But he holds on to manuscript.*) This reconstruction of the Springs . . .

ASLAKSEN. I realize, Your Honor, it does mean tremendous sacrifices for the stockholders . . .

PETER. Don't upset yourself. The first thing a Mayor learns is that the less wealthy can always be prevailed upon to demand a spirit of sacrifice for the public good.

ASLAKSEN. I'm glad you see that.

PETER. Oh, yes. Especially when it's the wealthy who are going to do the sacrificing. What you don't seem to understand, Mr. Aslaksen, is that so long as I am Mayor, any changes in those baths are going to be paid for by a municipal loan.

ASLAKSEN. A municipal . . . You mean you're going to tax the people for this?

PETER. Exactly.

HOVSTAD. But the Springs are a private corporation . . .

PETER. (*Sets cane on table.*) The corporation built Kirsten Springs out of its own money. If the people want them changed, the people naturally must pay the bill. The corporation is in no position to put out any more money. It simply can't do it.

ASLAKSEN. That's impossible. People will never stand for another tax. (*To* PETER.) Is this a fact, or your opinion?

PETER. It happens to be a fact. Plus another fact—you'll forgive me for talking about facts in a newspaper office—but don't forget that the Springs will take two years to make over. Two years without income for your small businessmen, Mr. Aslaksen, and a heavy new tax, besides. And all because . . . (*Throttling manuscript in his hand.*) because of this dream, this hallucination that we live in a pest-hole . . .

HOVSTAD. That's based on science . . .

43

PETER. (*Throwing manuscript on table.*) This is based on vindictiveness, on his hatred of authority, and nothing else. (*Pounds fist on manuscript.*) This is the mad dream of a man who is trying to blow up our way of life! It has nothing to do with reform or science or anything else but pure and simple destruction! And I intend to see to it that the people understand it exactly so!

ASLAKSEN. (*Hit by this.*) My God! Maybe . . . (*Crosses* PETER *to* R. *of* HOVSTAD, *takes* HOVSTAD D. L.) You sure you want to support this thing, Hovstad?

HOVSTAD. (*Nervously.*) Frankly, I'd never thought of it in quite that way. I mean . . . (*Crosses above* ASLAKSEN; *to* PETER.) When you think of it psychologically it's completely possible, of course, that the man is simply out to . . . I don't know what to say, Your Honor. I'd hate to hurt the town in any way . . . I never imagined we'd have to have a new tax.

PETER. You should have imagined it, because you're going to have to advocate it. Unless, of course, liberal and radical newspaper readers enjoy high taxes. . . . (*Takes own manuscript out of inside coat pocket.*) You'd know that better than I, of course. I happen to have here a brief story of the actual facts. It proves that with a little care, nobody need be harmed at all by the water. Of course, in time we'd have to make a few minor structural changes, and we'd pay for those.

HOVSTAD. May I see that?

PETER. I want you to study it, Mr. Hovstad, and see if you don't agree that . . . (BILLING *hurries in quickly from* U. L., *closing door, comes* D. *around back of table.*)

BILLING. Are you expecting the Doctor?

PETER. (*Alarmed, rising quickly, replacing manuscript in pocket.*) He's here?

BILLING. (*Motioning to street at* R.) He's just crossing the street. (ASLAKSEN *crosses quickly to* D. R. *door.*)

PETER. I'd rather not run into him here. How can I . . . ?

BILLING. (*Taking* PETER *to* D. L. *door.*) Right this way, sir. Hurry up. . . .

ASLAKSEN. (*At* R. *door, peeking.*) Hurry up!

PETER. (*Going out* D. L. *door with* BILLING.) Get him out of here right away!

HOVSTAD. (*Covering* STOCKMANN'S *manuscript with papers on table, sitting in* D. C. *chair.*) Do something, do something! (ASLAK-

44

SEN *rushes to* BILLING'S *desk, turns chair up, sits and becomes very, very busy, seating himself to cover hat.*)

STOCKMANN. (*Entering* D. R. *and crossing* C.) Any proofs yet? (*Looks at* HOVSTAD, *then at* ASLAKSEN.) I guess not, heh?

ASLAKSEN. (*Without turning.*) No, you can't expect them for some time.

STOCKMANN. You mind if I wait?

HOVSTAD. (*Trying to smile.*) No sense in that, Doctor; it'll be quite a while yet.

STOCKMANN. (*Laughing, places his hand on* HOVSTAD'S *back.*) Bear with me, Hovstad, I just can't wait to see it in print.

HOVSTAD. We're pretty busy, Doctor, so . . .

STOCKMANN. (*Starting for* D. R. *door.*) Don't let me hold you up. That's the way to be, busy, busy. We'll make this town shine like a jewel! (*Exits* D. R. *After a moment he returns.*) Just one thing, I . . .

HOVSTAD. Couldn't we talk some other time? We're very . . .

STOCKMANN. Two words. Just walking down the street now, I looked at the people, in the stores, driving the wagons, and suddenly I was . . . well, touched, you know? By their innocence, I mean. What I'm driving at is when this exposé breaks, they're liable to start making a saint out of me or something, and I . . . (*Moves to* ASLAKSEN.) Aslaksen, I want you to promise me that you're not going to try to get up any dinner for me, or . . .

ASLAKSEN. (*Rising.*) Doctor, there's no use concealing . . .

STOCKMANN. I knew it! Now look, I will simply not attend a dinner in my honor.

HOVSTAD. (*Rising.*) Doctor, I think it's time we . . . (CATHERINE *enters* D. R. *and crosses to* STOCKMANN.)

CATHERINE. I thought so! Thomas, I want you home. Now come. I want you to talk to Petra. (*She returns to* D. R. *door.*)

STOCKMANN. What happened? What are you doing here?

HOVSTAD. Something wrong, Mrs. Stockmann?

CATHERINE. (*Crossing to* HOVSTAD.) Doctor Stockmann is the father of three children, Mr. Hovstad!

STOCKMANN. Now look, dear, everybody knows that, what's the . . .

CATHERINE. (*Restraining at outburst at* STOCKMANN.) Nobody would believe it from the way you're dragging us into this disaster!

HOVSTAD. Oh, now, Mrs. Stockmann . . .

STOCKMANN. What disaster?

CATHERINE. (*To* HOVSTAD.) He treats you like a son and you want to make a fool of him.

HOVSTAD. (*Gives way,* CATHERINE *follows.*) I'm not making a . . .

STOCKMANN. Catherine, how can you accuse . . .

CATHERINE. (*To* HOVSTAD, *backs him to below table.*) He'll lose his job at the Springs, do you realize that? You print the article and they'll grind him up like a piece of flesh!

STOCKMANN. (*Putting hat on table.*) Catherine, you're embarrassing me! I beg your pardon, gentlemen . . .

CATHERINE. Mr. Hovstad, what are you up to?

STOCKMANN. I won't have you jumping at Hovstad, Catherine!

CATHERINE. (*To* STOCKMANN.) I want you home! This man is not your friend!

STOCKMANN. He is my friend—any man who shares my risk is my friend! You simply don't understand that as soon as this breaks, everybody in this town is going to come out in the streets . . . (*Picks up cane from table.*) and drive that gang of . . . (*He notices cane, recognizes it, looks at* HOVSTAD, *then* ASLAKSEN.) What's this? (*No reply. He looks from* ASLAKSEN *to desk, sees hat and picks it up on cane, comes D. As he goes to desk,* ASLAKSEN *crosses to D. of table,* CATHERINE *goes around L. and U. of table.*) What the hell is he doing here?

ASLAKSEN. All right, Doctor, now let's be calm and . . .

STOCKMANN. (*Crossing D. L.,* ASLAKSEN *and* HOVSTAD *give up,* CATHERINE *backs to D. R. end of table, looking at door.*) Where is he? What'd he do, talk you out of it? Hovstad! (*No reply.*) He won't get away with it; where'd you hide him? (*Opens door D. L.*)

ASLAKSEN. Be careful, Doctor! (PETER *enters D. L. and crosses D. R. C.* BILLING *enters D. L. and stands D. L., closes door.* PETER *is trying to hide his embarrassment.*)

STOCKMANN. (*Crossing to* PETER *at R. C.*) Well, Peter! Poisoning the water wasn't enough, you're working on the press now, eh?

PETER. My hat, please. And my stick. (STOCKMANN *puts on* PETER'S *hat.*) Now what's *this* nonsense? Take that off, that's official insignia!

STOCKMANN. I just wanted you to realize, Peter . . . (*Takes off hat.*) that anyone may wear this hat in a democracy, and . . . (*Handing him hat.*) that a free citizen is not afraid to touch it.

46

And as for the baton of command, Your Honor, it can pass from hand to hand. So don't gloat yet. (*Hands stick to* PETER.) The people haven't spoken. (*Turning to* HOVSTAD *and* ASLAKSEN.) And I have the people because I have the truth, my friends.

ASLAKSEN. (*Moving down.*) Doctor, we're not scientists; we can't judge whether your article is really true.

STOCKMANN. Then print it under my name; let *me* defend it!

HOVSTAD. (*Moving down.*) I'm not printing it. I'm not going to sacrifice this newspaper. When the whole story gets out the public is not going to stand for any changes in the Springs.

ASLAKSEN. His Honor just told us, Doctor. You see, there will have to be a new tax . . .

STOCKMANN. Ahhh! Yes. I see! That's why you're not scientists suddenly and can't decide if I'm telling the truth. Well, so.

HOVSTAD. Don't take that attitude. The point is . . .

STOCKMANN. (*Crossing to* ASLAKSEN; CATHERINE *gives* R.) The point, the point, oh, the point is going to fly through this town like an arrow, and I'm going to fire it! Will you print this article as a pamphlet? I'll pay for it.

ASLAKSEN. I'm not going to ruin this paper or this town. Doctor, for the sake of your family . . .

CATHERINE. (*Picking up hat from table, moving* D. *to* L. *of* STOCKMANN.) You can leave his family out of this, Mr. Aslaksen. God help me, I think you people are horrible!

STOCKMANN. My article, if you don't mind!

ASLAKSEN. (*Giving it to him.*) Doctor, you won't get it printed in this town.

PETER. Can't you forget it? (*Indicating* HOVSTAD *and* ASLAKSEN.) Can't you see now that everybody . . . ?

STOCKMANN. Your Honor, I can't forget it, and you will never forget it as long as you live. I'm going to call a mass meeting and I . . .

PETER. And who is going to rent you a hall?

STOCKMANN. Then I will take a drum and go from—(*Crosses to* PETER.) street to street proclaiming that the springs are befouled and poison is rotting the body politic!

PETER. And I believe you really are that mad!

STOCKMANN. (*Waving manuscript in his hand.*) Mad? Oh, my brother, you haven't even heard me raise my voice yet. Catherine? (*He holds out his* L. *arm, she takes it. They cross* PETER *and go stiffly out* D. R. PETER *shakes his head regretfully, reaches into pocket, takes out his own manuscript, looks at* ASLAKSEN, *who crosses and takes it.* ASLAKSEN *quickly looks at* HOVSTAD, *who crosses and takes it.* HOVSTAD *looks at* BILLING, *who crosses and takes it, gestures a salute and exits* U. L. PETER *acknowledges* BILLING'S *salute as)*

FAST CURTAIN

ACT II

SCENE 2

A room in CAPTAIN HORSTER'S *house. The room is bare, as though unused for a long time. There is a platform* R. *of* C. *with a chair and a small table on it.* R. *of platform are two small chairs.* D. L. *is a highbacked chair. Two windows with shutters are in back wall. A shelf is between them. There is a doorway* D. R. *and an archway in* L. *wall, which leads to a doorway.*

At rise, the stage is empty. CAPTAIN HORSTER *enters from* R., *carrying a pitcher of water on a tray with two glasses. As he is putting these on the table,* BILLING *enters* L.

BILLING. Captain Horster?

HORSTER. *(Tidying up platform table, doesn't see* BILLING.) Oh, come in. I don't have enough chairs for a lot of people, so I decided not to have chairs at all.

BILLING. My name is Billing. Don't you remember, at the Doctor's house?

HORSTER. *(A little coldly.)* Oh, yes, sure—I've been so busy I didn't recognize you. *(Crosses* BILLING *to* U. L. C. *window, looks out.)* Why don't those people come inside?

BILLING. I don't know. I guess they're waiting for the Mayor or somebody important so they can be sure it's respectable in here. I wanted to ask you a question before it begins, Captain. (HORSTER *crosses to* BILLING.) Why are you lending your house for this? I

48

never heard of you connected with anything political.

HORSTER. I'll answer that. I travel most of the year . . . Did you ever travel?

BILLING. Not abroad, no.

HORSTER. Well, I've been in a lot of places where people aren't allowed to say unpopular things. Did you know that?

BILLING. Sure, I've read about it.

HORSTER. (Simply.) Well, I don't like it. (Starts to go out D. R.)

BILLING. (Dutifully writes down " doesn't like it.") One more question. (HORSTER stops.) What's your opinion about the Doctor's proposition to rebuild the Springs?

HORSTER. (After a moment.) Don't understand a thing about it. (HORSTER sees some people in room U. L., through door.) Come in. Come in. (NANSEN, HENRIK and EDVARD enter L. and cross U. C. BILLING crosses D. L.) I don't have enough chairs, so you'll just have to stand. (HORSTER goes out D. R.)

HENRIK. (As soon as HORSTER is off.) Try the horn.

EDVARD. No, let him start to talk first.

NANSEN. (Taking out horn.) Wait'll they hear this! I could blow your moustache off with this! (HORSTER has re-entered R., carrying two more glasses. Stops on seeing horn.)

HORSTER. (Setting things on table.) I don't want any rough-house, you hear me? (CATHERINE and PETRA enter L.) Come in. I've got chairs just for you. (As the women move to HORSTER at C. PETRA crosses U. of CATHERINE and reaches HORSTER first.)

CATHERINE. (Nervously.) There's quite a crowd on the sidewalk. Why don't they come in?

HORSTER. I suppose they're waiting for the Mayor.

PETRA. Are all those people on his side?

HORSTER. Who knows? People are bashful . . . (BILLING crosses to ladies at C.) and it's so unusual to come to a meeting like this, I suppose they . . .

BILLING. (Taking off hat.) Good evening, ladies. (CATHERINE and PETRA don't look at him.) I don't blame you for not speaking. I just wanted to say I don't think this is going to be a place for ladies tonight.

CATHERINE. I don't remember asking your advice, Mr. Billing.

BILLING. I'm not as bad as you think, Mrs. Stockmann.

CATHERINE. Then why did you print the Mayor's statement and not a word about my husband's report? Nobody's had a chance to find out what he really stands for. Why, everybody on the street there is against him already!

BILLING. If we printed his report it only would have hurt your husband.

CATHERINE. Mr. Billing, I've never said this to anyone in my life, but I think you're a liar. (*Suddenly* NANSEN, *who is directly behind* CATHERINE, *lets out a blast on his horn. The women jump.* HORSTER *moves the women* D. L. C., *then goes* U. *to the three men who have moved* U. L. C.)

HORSTER. You do that once more and I'll throw you out of here! (PETER *enters* L., *briskly and crosses to women. Behind him are* HEDVIG, GEORG, *and* GUNNAR, *who cross* D. R. *in front of chair.* BILLING *crosses to the men.*)

PETER. (*Nodding.*) Catherine? Petra? (HORSTER *crosses* D. *to* R. *of* PETER. GUNNAR *tries to get* EDVARD'S *attention.*)

PETRA. Good evening.

PETER. Why so coldly? He wanted a meeting and he's got it. (*To* HORSTER.) Isn't he here? (*A* DRUNK *crosses to* U. L. *group.* HEDVIG *and* GUNNAR *watch him.*)

HORSTER. The Doctor is going around town to be sure that there's a good attendance. (*He crosses* U. C. *and watches* DRUNK.)

PETER. Fair enough. By the way, Petra, did you paint that poster —the one somebody stuck on the town hall?

PETRA. If you can call it a painting, yes.

PETER. You know I could arrest you, it's against the law to deface the Town Hall.

PETRA. (*Holding out hands for handcuffs.*) Well, here I am.

CATHERINE. If you arrest her, Peter, I'll never speak to you!

PETER. (*Crossing* D. L., *laughing.*) Catherine, you have no sense of humor! (*He sees* HEDVIG, GUNNAR *and* GEORG *in front of his chair. They dart* U. *and he sits.* DRUNK, *egged on by the* U. L. *group, crosses* D. *to* HORSTER.)

DRUNK. Say, friend, who's runnin'! Who's the candidate?!

HORSTER. You're drunk, Mister. Now get out of here.

DRUNK. There's no law says a man who's drunk can't vote!

HORSTER. (*Crossing* DRUNK *in front of him, pushes* DRUNK *to* L. *door as* CROWD *laughs.*) Get out of here, get out . . .

DRUNK. I wanna vote! I got a right to vote! (ASLAKSEN *has entered* L. *and* HORSTER *pushes* DRUNK *into him.* ASLAKSEN *recoils upstage,* HORSTER *pushes* DRUNK *out door* L.)

ASLAKSEN. (*Hurriedly and covertly crossing* D. *to* PETER.) Your Honor, (*Indicates* L. *door.*) he's . . .

STOCKMANN. (*Offstage.*) Right this way, gentlemen! (HOVSTAD *enters* L., *looks around, sees* PETER, *comes* D. *to* L. *of* ASLAKSEN.) In you go, come on, fellows . . . (PAUL *and* KNUT *enter* L., *followed by* STOCKMANN. *Then* TORA, PETER *and* FINN *enter* L. GUNNAR *crosses to* R. *of* HEDVIG *and* HANS, *who are in front of platform.*) Sorry no chairs, gentlemen, but we couldn't get a hall, y'know, so just relax, it won't take long. (STOCKMANN *crosses* C., *sees* PETER.) Glad you're here, Peter!

PETER. Wouldn't miss it for the world.

STOCKMANN. (*Crossing to* CATHERINE *and* PETRA, *taking off hat and coat, giving them to* PETRA.) How do you feel, Catherine?

CATHERINE. Just promise me, don't lose your temper . . . (STOCKMANN *helps them to chairs.* CATHERINE *sits in* R. *chair,* PETRA *in* R. *chair. While* HORSTER *is looking* R. DRUNK *enters* L. *and crosses* D. R. C.)

DRUNK. Look, if you ain't votin', what the hell's going on here!

HORSTER. (*Starting after him.*) Did I tell you to get out of here?

DRUNK. (*Imperiously.*) Don't push.

PETER. (*Rising.*) I order you to get out of here and stay out!

DRUNK. (*Imperiously.*) I don't like the tone of your voice! And if you don't watch your step I'm gonna tell the Mayor right now and he'll throw yiz all in the jug! (*Crowd is laughing,* DRUNK *turns to them.*) What're you, revolution here?! (*Amidst loud laughter,* DRUNK *turns and walks out* L., *immensely pleased with himself.*)

STOCKMANN. (*Mounting platform, quieting crowd.*) All right, gentlemen, we might as well begin. Quiet down, please. (*Crowd moves in* L. STOCKMANN *looks at* CATHERINE, *then at crowd.*) The issue is very simple . . .

ASLAKSEN. We haven't elected a chairman, Doctor.

STOCKMANN. I'm sorry, Mr. Aslaksen, this isn't a meeting; I advertised a lecture and I . . .

HENRIK. (*Raising hand.*) I came to a meeting, Doctor, there's got to be some kind of control here.

STOCKMANN. What do you mean, control . . . what is there to control?

HEDVIG. Sure, let him speak, this is no meeting!

EDVARD. (*Stepping to* PETER.) Your Honor, why don't you take charge of this . . . ?

STOCKMANN. Just a minute now . . .

EDVARD. (*Crossing* L. *to in front of* HEDVIG.) Somebody responsible has got to take charge . . . (*To* HEDVIG.) There's a big difference of opinion here . . . (*Returning* L. *of* GUNNAR.)

STOCKMANN. What makes you so sure? You don't even know yet what I'm going to say.

NANSEN. I've got a pretty good idea what you're going to say and I don't like it! If a man doesn't like it here let him go where it suits him better, we don't want any trouble-makers here! (*A low grunt of assent from crowd.* STOCKMANN *looks at them.*)

STOCKMANN. Now look, friend, you don't know anything about me . . .

NANSEN. We know plenty about you, Stockmann.

STOCKMANN. From what, from the newspapers? How do you know I don't like this town? (*Holds up notes.*) I'm here to save the life of this town.

PETER. (*Rising quickly.*) Now just a minute, Doctor. (*Crowd quickly becomes silent from* L. *to* R.) I think the democratic thing to do is to elect a chairman.

EDVARD. (*Quickly raising his hand.*) I nominate the Mayor!

NANSEN. (*Quickly raising his hand.*) Second the Mayor!

PETER. No, no, no. That wouldn't be fair. We want a neutral person. I suggest Mr. Aslaksen who has always . . .

HEDVIG. I came to a lecture, I didn't . . .

NANSEN. (*To* HEDVIG.) What're you afraid of a fair fight? (*To* PETER.) Second Mr. Aslaksen! (*Crowd assents: "Very good choice," etc.*)

STOCKMANN. All right, if that's your pleasure. I just want to remind you that the reason I arranged for this lecture was that I have a very important message for you people and . . . (ASLAKSEN *crosses* D. C.; STOCKMANN *gets off platform.*) I couldn't get it into the press and nobody would rent me a hall. (*To* PETER.) I just hope I'll be given time to speak here. (*To* ASLAKSEN.) Mr. Aslaksen? (*The crowd applauds* ASLAKSEN, *who mounts platform.* STOCKMANN *crosses to between* PETRA *and* CATHERINE. KNUT *crosses to* R. *of platform.* NANSEN *crosses and talks to* BILLING. HOVSTAD *crosses* R. *and talks to* PETER. FINN *crosses* D. *to* L. *of* EDVARD. KIIL *enters* L. *and stands just* R. *of* GABRIEL.)

ASLAKSEN. I just have one word before we start. Whatever is said tonight, please remember, the highest civic virtue is moderation. (*He can't help turning to* STOCKMANN, *then looks over to* PETER.) Now if anybody wants to speak . . . (DRUNK *enters* L. *suddenly and crosses* C.)

DRUNK. I heard that! Since when you allowed to electioneer at the polls? (*Crowd pushes him back to door* L. *amid laughter.*) I'm gonna report this to the Mayor, goddammit! (STOCKMANN *crosses* D. L., *looks after* DRUNK.)

ASLAKSEN. Quiet, please, quiet. (*Complete quiet.*) Does anybody want the floor? (STOCKMANN *raises his hand but* PETER *also raises his, almost imperceptibly.*)

PETER. Mr. Chairman!

ASLAKSEN. (*Quickly.*) His Honor the Mayor will address the meeting. (*Great applause.* STOCKMANN *returns to his position* L. *of* PETRA. PETER *rises and crosses to platform, which he mounts.* EDVARD *pulls* GUNNAR *to get better view of* PETER. BILLING *crosses to* D. C. *edge of platform as* HENRIK *goes* U. L. C. *to talk to* NANSEN. KIIL *sits in the Mayor's chair,* D. R. HOVSTAD *crosses to behind* BILLING.)

PETER. Gentlemen, there's no reason to take very long to settle this tonight and return to our ordinary calm and peaceful life. Here's the issue: Doctor Stockmann, my brother—and believe me, it's not easy to say this—has decided to destroy Kirsten Springs, our Health Institute . . . (*Crowd is dead quiet.*)

STOCKMANN. Peter!

ASLAKSEN. Let the Mayor continue, please. There mustn't be any interruptions.

PETER. He has a long and very involved way of going about it, but that's the brunt of it, believe me.

NANSEN. (*Rather quietly.*) Then what're we wasting time for? Run him out of town! (HENRIK "*plots*" *with* NANSEN. *Others agree,* HEDVIG *disagrees.*)

PETER. Now wait a minute. I want no violence here. I want you to understand his motives. He is a man, always has been, who is never happy unless he is badgering authority, ridiculing authority, destroying authority. He wants to attack the Springs so he can prove that the Administration blundered in the construction.

STOCKMANN. (*To* ASLAKSEN.) May I speak, I . . . ?

ASLAKSEN. The Mayor's not finished. (STOCKMANN *turns and steps* D. *distractedly.*)

PETER. Thank you. Now there are a number of people here who seem to feel that the Doctor has a right to say anything he pleases. After all, we are a democratic country. Now God knows, in ordinary times, I'd agree a hundred percent with anybody's right to say anything. But these are not ordinary times. Nations have crises and so do towns. There are ruins of nations and there are ruins of towns all over the world, and they were wrecked by people who in the guise of reform and pleading for justice and so on, broke down all authority and left only revolution and chaos.

STOCKMANN. (*Crossing* D. L. *of platform.*) What the hell are you talking about!

ASLAKSEN. (*As crowd begins to murmur.*) I'll have to insist, Doctor . . .

STOCKMANN. I called a lecture, I didn't invite him to attack me. (*Crosses to crowd.*) He's got the press and every hall in town to attack me and I've got nothing but this room tonight. (*Crowd snarls and advances on* STOCKMANN.)

ASLAKSEN. I don't think you're making a very good impression, Doctor. (*Assenting laughter and catcalls.* DRUNK *whistles loudly from arch* L. HORSTER *quiets him.* HOVSTAD *crosses* D. *then* U. *to* BILLING. GUNNAR *and* EDVARD *cross to* GABRIEL *to deplore situation.* STOCKMANN *backs away from crowd, dismayed, goes up to confer with family.* ASLAKSEN *rings and calls for quiet, finally gets it.*) Please continue, Your Honor.

PETER. Now this is our crisis. We know what this town was without our Institute. We could barely afford to keep the streets in condition; it was a dead, third-rate hamlet. Today we're just on the verge of becoming internationally known as a resort. I predict that within five years the income of every man in this room will be immensely greater. (HENRIK *chuckles at this prospect.*) I predict that our schools will be bigger and better; and in time this town will be crowded with fine carriages; (GABRIEL *beams at* KIIL, *who glowers back.*) great homes will be built here, first-class stores will open all along Main Street. (*Crowd murmurs in appreciation.*) I predict that if we were not defamed and maliciously attacked we will some day be one of the richest and most beautiful resort towns in the world. (*General applause.*) There are your choices. Now all you've got to do is ask yourselves a simple question—has any one of us the right, the "democratic" right as they like to call it, to pick at minor flaws in the Springs, to exaggerate the most picayune faults . . . (*Cries of "No, no!"*) and to attempt to publish these defamations for the whole world to see? We live or die on what the outside world thinks of us! I believe there is a line that must be drawn, and if a man decides to cross that line, we the people must finally take him by the collar and declare, "You cannot say that." (*An uproar of assent.* HENRIK *and* NANSEN *cross* D. *after* STOCKMANN. BILLING *and* HOVSTAD *forcibly stop them and they return* U. R. C. EDVARD *reaches and pulls* GUNNAR *back* L. *out of danger.* GABRIEL *crosses to* FINN, *takes him* U. L. C. HORSTER *crosses* D. L.) All right, then. I think we all understand each other. Mr. Aslaksen, I move that Doctor Stockmann be prohibited from reading his report at this meeting. (*Ovation.* PETER *returns to his chair* D. R., *accepting the handshakes and plaudits of crowd. He finds* KIIL *sitting in his chair,* KIIL *disgustedly rises and scornfully gives* PETER *his place.* STOCKMANN *is behind his family at* L., *talking to them.* ASLAKSEN *is ringing bell and finally quiets the enthusiasm.*)

ASLAKSEN. Quiet, please! Please, now! I think we can proceed to the vote. (PETRA *claps* STOCKMANN *on the back.*)

STOCKMANN. Well, aren't you going to let me speak at all?

ASLAKSEN. Doctor, we are just about to vote on that question.

STOCKMANN. But damn it, man, I've got a right to . . .

PETRA. (*Moving behind* STOCKMANN.) Point of order, Father!

STOCKMANN. (*Remembering.*) Yes, point of order!

ASLAKSEN. Yes, Doctor? (STOCKMANN, *at a loss, turns to* PETRA *for further instruction.*)

PETRA. You want to discuss the motion.

STOCKMANN. That's right, damn it. I want to discuss the motion!

ASLAKSEN. Ah . . . (*Glances at* PETER, *who nods.*) All right, go ahead. (PETRA *sits.*)

STOCKMANN. (*Moving to* D. *of platform.*) Now listen. (*Pointing to* PETER.) He talks and he talks and he talks, but not a word about the facts. (*Holding up papers.*)

HENRIK. (*Snarling.*) We don't want to hear any more about the water!

NANSEN. You're just trying to blow up everything!

STOCKMANN. Well, judge for yourselves. Let me read . . . (*Crowd calls, "No, no, no." This rapidly builds into the biggest,* noisiest reaction: *shouting, horns blowing, bell ringing. Crutches and canes are waved in the air.* PETRA *and* CATHERINE *rise.*)

ASLAKSEN (*Ringing for quiet.*) Please, please now, quiet. We can't have this uproar! (*Quiet finally comes.*) I think, Doctor, that the majority wants to take the vote before you start to speak. If they so will, you can speak, otherwise . . . majority rules, you won't deny that.

STOCKMANN. (*Turns and tosses notes to* PETRA.) Don't bother voting. I understand everything now. Can I have a few minutes?

PETER. (*Rising.*) Mr. Chairman . . .

STOCKMANN. (*Crossing* D. C.; *to* PETER.) I won't mention the Institute. (*Crowd recoils before him.*) I have a new discovery that's a thousand times more important than all the institutes in the world. (*To* ASLAKSEN.) May I have the platform?

ASLAKSEN. (*Looking over crowd to* PETER.) I don't see how we can deny him that as long as he confines himself to . . . (*Crowd discusses* ASLAKSEN'S *decision.* HOVSTAD *fades* D. R. C.)

STOCKMANN. The Springs are not the subject. (*He mounts platform.* ASLAKSEN, CATHERINE, *and* PETRA *sit.* TORA *crosses to* U. *of* PETER; FINN *crosses* U. R.; BILLING *and* HOVSTAD *are* D. R. C.; HORSTER *crosses* L. C.; GABRIEL *crosses to in front of* PETER; EDVARD *and* GUNNAR *cross* U. R. C.; PAUL *crosses* D. C.; GEORG *puts bag of raisins in pocket.*) Before I go into my subject, I want to congratulate the " liberals " and " radicals " among us— like Mr. Hovstad . . . (BILLING *takes notes during* STOCKMANN'S *speech.*)

HOVSTAD. What do you mean, radical! Where's your evidence to call me a radical! (DRUNK *enters* L. *and leans against the arch.*)

STOCKMANN. You got me there. There isn't any evidence. I guess there never really was. I just wanted to congratulate you on your self-control tonight—you who have fought in every parlor for the principle of free speech these many years.

HOVSTAD. I believe in democracy. When my readers are overwhelmingly against something, I'm not going to impose my will on the majority.

STOCKMANN. You have begun my remarks, Mr. Hovstad. (*Turns to crowd.*) Gentlemen, Mrs. Stockmann, Miss Stockmann, tonight I was struck by a sudden flash of light, a discovery second to none. But before I tell it to you, a little story. (*Slight improvisation of exasperation.*) I put in a good many years in the North of our country. Up there the rulers of the world are the great seal and the gigantic squadrons of duck. Man lives on ice, huddled together in a little pile of stone. His whole life consists of grubbing for food. Nothing more. He can barely speak his own language. And it came to me one day that it was romantic and sentimental for a man of my education to be tending these people. They had not yet reached the stage where they needed a doctor. If the truth were to be told, a veterinary would be more in order. (*A murmur of displeasure works through crowd.*)

BILLING. Is that the way you refer to decent, hard-working people!

STOCKMANN. I expected that, my friend, but don't think you can fog up my brain with that magic word, the People! Not any more! Just because there is a mass of organisms with the human shape . . . (*Crowd reacts to this insult.*) they do not automatically become a People. That *honor* has to be *earned!* Nor does one automatically become " A Man " by having human shape, and living in a house, and feeding one's face—and agreeing with one's neighbors. (*Slight reaction to this insult.*) That name *also* has to be earned. (*Crowd becomes quiet by the force of his words.*) Now, when I came to my conclusions about the Springs . . .

PETER. (*Rising.*) You have no right to . . .

STOCKMANN. That's a picayune thing to catch me on a word, Peter, I'm not going into the Springs. (*To crowd.*) When I became convinced of my theory about the water, the authorities moved in at once, and I said to myself, I will fight them to the death because . . .

NANSEN. (*Quietly.*) What're you trying to make, a revolution here? (*To* GUNNAR.) He's a revolutionist!

STOCKMANN. (*Almost pleading to* NANSEN.) Let me finish! (*To crowd.*) I thought to myself—the majority, I have the majority! And let me tell you, friends, it was a grand feeling. Because the reason I came back to this place of my birth was that I wanted to give my education to this town, I loved it, so I spent months without pay or encouragement and dreamed up the whole project of the Springs. And why? Not as my brother says, so that fine carriages could crowd our streets, but so that we might cure the sick, so that we might meet people from all over the world and learn from them, and become broader and more civilized—in other words, more like Men, more like A People.

EDVARD. You don't like anything about this town, do you?

NANSEN. Admit it, you're a revolutionist, aren't you? Admit it!

STOCKMANN. I don't admit it! I proclaim it now! I am in revolt against the age-old lie that the majority is *always* right! (*Crowd's reaction is astonished, stunned.*)

HOVSTAD. He's an aristocrat all of a sudden!

STOCKMANN. And more! I tell you now, that the majority is always wrong, and in this way!

PETER. Have you lost your mind! Stop talking before . . .

STOCKMANN. Was the majority right when they stood by while Jesus was crucified? (*Silence.*) Was the majority right when they refused to believe that the earth moved round the sun, and let Galileo be driven to his knees like a dog? It takes fifty years for the majority to be right. The majority is never right until it *does* right.

HOVSTAD. I want to state right now, that although I've been this man's friend and I've eaten at his table many times, I now cut myself off from him absolutely. (*Starts to leave* U. R.; GABRIEL, BILLING *and* FINN *restrain him.* EDVARD *and* GUNNAR *start off,* STOCKMANN'S *pleas bring them back.*)

STOCKMANN. Answer me this! Please, one more moment! A platoon of soldiers is walking down a road toward the enemy. Every one of them is convinced he is on the right road, the safe road. But two miles ahead stands one lonely man, the outpost. He sees that this road is dangerous, that his comrades are walking into a trap. He runs back, he finds the platoon. Isn't it clear that this man must have the right to warn the majority, to argue with the majority, to fight with the majority if he believes he has the truth? Before many can know something, *one* must know it! (*His passion has made a silence.*) It's always the same. Rights are sacred until it hurts for somebody to use them. I beg you now—I realize the cost is great, the inconvenience is great, the risk is great that other towns will get the jump on us while we're rebuilding . . .

PETER. Aslaksen, he's not allowed to . . .

STOCKMANN. Let me prove it to you! The water is poisoned!

NANSEN. (*Crosses to below platform, waving fist in air,* PETRA *rises and crosses to give* STOCKMANN *his report, but bumps into* NANSEN.) One more word about poison and I'm gonna take you outside! (*Crowd surges forward.* CATHERINE *pulls* PETRA *back* D. L. *Bell is ringing, crowd is roaring. Canes and crutches are waved in the air. Even the* DRUNK, *who has dozed off while leaning in archway* L., *starts to fight an imaginary opponent. All are violent*

" for the good of the town." KIIL *takes this all in, then darts away off* L. HENRIK *has crossed, and is arguing with the women.* HEDVIG *screams when crowd moves forward, then runs* R. C. *with* HANS; GUNNAR *crosses to her.* HORSTER, *who has been pulling men out of the crowd, sees* HENRIK *with the two women and crosses to get him away, then stays* D. L. *to protect the women.* PETER *is standing* R. C., *watching all this.*)

PETER. That's enough! Now stop it! Quiet! There is not going to be any violence here!! (*People in the crowd look at* PETER *and become quiet. After a moment.*) Doctor, come down and give Mr. Aslaksen the platform.

STOCKMANN. I'm not through yet.

PETER. Come down or I will not be responsible for what happens.

CATHERINE. I'd like to go home; come on, Tom.

PETER. I move the Chairman order the speaker to leave the platform.

EDVARD. Sit down!

NANSEN. Get off that platform! (*Others join in.*) } (*Together.*)

STOCKMANN. All right. Then I'll take this to out-of-town newspapers until the whole country is warned . . .

PETER. You wouldn't dare!

HOVSTAD. (*Breaking away* R. C.) You're trying to ruin this town, that's all, trying to ruin it.

STOCKMANN. You are trying to build a town on a morality so rotten that it will infect the country and the world! If the only way you can prosper is this murder of freedom and truth, then I say with all my heart—let it be destroyed, let the people perish! (*He jumps down from rear of platform and crosses to his family* D. R. HORSTER *helps him with his hat and coat. Crowd turns to* PETER *for action.*)

NANSEN. Arrest him!

HENRIK and FINN. He's a traitor! Traitor! }

GABRIEL. Revolution!

ASLAKSEN. (*Ringing for quiet.*) I would like to submit the following resolution: The people assembled here tonight, decent and patriotic citizens, in defense of their town and their country, declare, that Doctor Stockmann, Medical Officer of the Springs, is an enemy of the people and of his community.

CATHERINE. That's not true! He loves this town!

STOCKMANN. You damned fools, you fools! (*Crowd advances on* STOCKMANN.)

ASLAKSEN. (*Shouting over the din.*) Is there anyone against this motion? Anyone against? (*Crowd becomes quiet. After a moment.*)

HORSTER. (*Raises hand.*) I am. (*Crowd backs away.*)

ASLAKSEN. One?

DRUNK. (*Raises his hand, sleepily.*) Me, too! You can't do without a Doctor . . . (*Everyone looks back at* ASLAKSEN.) Anybody'll tell you . . .

ASLAKSEN. Anyone else? With all votes against two, this assembly formally declares Doctor Thomas Stockmann to be the people's enemy. In the future, all dealings with him by decent, patriotic citizens will be on that basis. The meeting is adjourned. (*Applause.* ASLAKSEN *and* BILLING *and* HOVSTAD *cross* D. R. *to* PETER; HOVSTAD *helps him on with coat.* HEDVIG *and* GEORG *cross* C.)

STOCKMANN. (*Stepping to* HORSTER.) Captain, do you have room for us on your ship to America?

HORSTER. Any time you say, Doctor. (NANSEN *steps* D., *looks at* HORSTER, *then crosses* U. R.)

STOCKMANN. Catherine! (*She takes his* R. *arm.*) Petra? (*She takes his* L. *arm. They start for door* U. L. *Crowd falls silent, a gauntlet is formed.* HEDVIG *looks at the three, then hides her boy's head, ashamed, and turns away herself. As the three start to move:*)

NANSEN. Doctor! (*Slight pause.*) You'd better get on that ship soon.

CATHERINE. (*Quickly.*) Let's go out the back door . . .

HORSTER. Right this way . . .

STOCKMANN. No, no! No back doors! (*To crowd.*) I don't want to mislead anybody—the enemy of the people is not finished in this town—not quite yet! And if anybody thinks . . .

HENRIK. (*Suddenly.*) Traitor! (*Quickly the noise builds.*)

EDVARD. Enemy! Enemy!

NANSEN. Throw him in the river! Come on, throw } (*Together.*)
him in the river!

(*Out of the noise, a chant emerges, soon the whole crowd is calling, "Enemy! Enemy!" stamping their feet on last syllable. Through the two lines the* STOCKMANNS, *erect, move. Crowd is snapping at them like animals.* STOCKMANN, PETER, BILLING, ASLAKSEN *and* HOVSTAD *are seen watching,* D. L. *The whole stage throbs with the chant, "Enemy, enemy, enemy."*)

CURTAIN

ACT III

SCENE: *Same as* ACT I, SCENE 1.
The following morning. Windows at R. *are broken. Disorder. There are small rocks around the room:* D. C.*, under* C. *chair, under the* R. C. *chair, and in front of bay window.*
STOCKMANN *enters* D. L. *with robe over shirt and trousers, closes door. It's cold in the house. He picks up a stone from* D. C.*, sets it on table where there is a little pile of rocks.*

STOCKMANN. Catherine! Tell what's-her-name there's still some rocks to pick up in here!
CATHERINE. (*Off* U. L.) She's not finished sweeping up the glass! (STOCKMANN *bends down to get another stone under a chair when a rock is thrown through one of the last remaining panes. He whirls around and rushes to* U. *of window, looks out.* CATHERINE *runs in from dining-room door and crosses to* STOCKMANN. *They put their arms round each other.*) You all right?!
STOCKMANN. (*Looking out window.*) A little boy. Look at him run. (*Picking up stone in front of window.*) How fast the poison spreads—even to the children. (*Crosses and sets rock on* R. C. *table.*)
CATHERINE. (*Looking out window, has chill.*) It's hard to believe this is the same town . . .
STOCKMANN. I'm going to keep these like sacred relics. I'll put them in my will. I want the boys to have these in their homes to look at every day. (*Shudders.*) Cold in here. Why hasn't what's-her-name got the glazier here?
CATHERINE. (*Turns to him, steps* D.) She's getting him . . .
STOCKMANN. She's been getting him for two hours. We'll freeze to death in here. (*Pulls muffler around neck.*)
CATHERINE. (*Unwillingly.*) He won't come here, Tom.
STOCKMANN. No! The glazier's afraid to fix my windows?
CATHERINE. You don't realize . . . people don't like to be pointed out. He's got neighbors, I suppose, and . . . (*A knock on* U. R. *door.*) Is that someone at the door? (*She goes to* U. R. *door.*

61

STOCKMANN *picks up stone under* R. *chair.* CATHERINE *returns.*)
Letter for you.
STOCKMANN. (*Taking and opening it.*) What's this now?
CATHERINE. (*Picking up stone under* C. *chair.*) I don't know how
we're going to do any shopping with everybody ready to bite my
head off . . .
STOCKMANN. Well, what do you know! We're evicted!
CATHERINE. Oh, no!
STOCKMANN. He hates to do it, but with public opinion what it
is . . .
CATHERINE. (*Frightened, crosses* U. C.) Maybe we shouldn't have
let the boys go to school today?
STOCKMANN. (*Crosses* U. R. *around table to* U. C.) Now don't get
all frazzled again . . .
CATHERINE. But the landlord is such a nice man. If he's got to
throw us out the town must be ready to murder us!
STOCKMANN. Just calm down, will you? (*Leads her to* C. *chair,
sits, pulls her down on his* L. *knee.*) We'll go to America and the
whole thing'll be like a dream . . .
CATHERINE. But I don't want to go to America. . . . (*Noticing
his pants.*) When did this get torn?
STOCKMANN. Must've been last night . . .
CATHERINE. Your best pants!
STOCKMANN. Well, it shows you, that's all. Man goes out to fight
for the truth should never wear his best pants. (*She half-laughs.*)
Stop worrying, will you? You'll sew them up and in no time at
all we'll be three thousand miles away . . .
CATHERINE. But how do you know it'll be any different there?
STOCKMANN. I don't know, it just seems to me in a big country
like that, the spirit must be bigger. Still, I suppose they must have
the solid majority there, too? I don't know, at least there must be
more room to hide there.
CATHERINE. Think about it more, will you? I'd hate to go half
around the world and find out we're in the same place.
STOCKMANN. You know, Catherine, I don't think I'm ever going to
forget the face of that crowd last night.
CATHERINE. (*Puts shawl around him.*) Don't think about it . . .
STOCKMANN. Some of them had their teeth bared, like animals in
a pack. And who leads them? Men who call themselves liberals!
Radicals! (*She looks around at furniture, figuring.*) The crowd

lets out one roar and where are they—my liberal friends! I bet if I walked down the street now not one of them would admit he ever met me! It's hard to believe, it's . . . Are you listening to me?

CATHERINE. I was just wondering what we'll ever do with this furniture if we go to America?

STOCKMANN. Don't you ever listen when I talk, dear?

CATHERINE. Why must I listen? I know you're right. (PETRA *enters* U. R. CATHERINE *sees her, rises.*) Petra! Why aren't you in school?

STOCKMANN. (*Rises, as* PETRA *crosses, steps back a little.*) What's the matter? (PETRA *crosses* D., *then* L. *to* STOCKMANN *at* C.; CATHERINE *comes* D. *a step and watches.* PETRA *kisses* STOCKMANN.)

PETRA. I'm fired.

CATHERINE. They wouldn't!

PETRA. As of two weeks from now. But I couldn't bear to stay there.

STOCKMANN. (*Shocked.*) Mrs. Busk fired you?

CATHERINE. Who'd ever imagine she could do such a thing?

PETRA. It hurt her. I could see it, because we've always agreed so about things. But she didn't dare do anything else . . .

STOCKMANN. The glazier doesn't dare fix the windows, the landlord doesn't dare let us stay on . . .

PETRA. The landlord!

STOCKMANN. Evicted, darling! Oh, God, on the wreckage of all the civilizations in the world there ought to be a big sign—" They Didn't Dare! "

PETRA. I really can't blame her, Father, she showed me three letters she got this morning . . .

STOCKMANN. From whom?

PETRA. They weren't signed . . .

STOCKMANN. Oh, naturally. The big patriots with their anonymous indignation, scrawling out the darkness of their minds onto dirty little slips of paper—that's morality, and *I'm* the traitor! What'd the letters say?

PETRA. Well, one of them was from somebody who said that he'd heard at the club that somebody who visits this house said I had radical opinions about certain things.

STOCKMANN. Oh, wonderful! Somebody heard that somebody heard that *she* heard that *he* heard!—Catherine, pack as soon as you can. I feel as though vermin were crawling all over me. (*He starts to door* D. L. HORSTER *enters* U. R. *immediately and crosses* D. R.)

HORSTER. Good morning!

STOCKMANN. (*Crossing to* HORSTER D. R. C.) Captain! You're just the man I want to see.

HORSTER. I thought I'd see how you all were . . .

CATHERINE. That's awfully nice of you, Captain . . . (*Stepping down and crossing to* L. *of* STOCKMANN.) and I want to thank you for seeing us through the crowd last night.

PETRA. Did you get home all right? We hated to leave you alone with that mob.

HORSTER. Oh, nothing to it. In a storm, there's just one thing to remember—it will pass.

STOCKMANN. Unless it kills you.

HORSTER. (*After a moment.*) You mustn't let yourself get too bitter.

STOCKMANN. I'm trying, I'm trying. But I don't guarantee how I'll feel when I try to walk down the street with " Traitor " branded on my forehead.

CATHERINE. Don't think about it. $\left.\begin{array}{l}\end{array}\right\}$ (*Together.*)
HORSTER. Ah, what's a word?

STOCKMANN. A word can be like a needle sticking in your heart, Captain. It can dig and corrode like an acid, until you become what they want you to be—really an enemy of the people.

HORSTER. You mustn't ever let that happen, Doctor.

STOCKMANN. Frankly, I don't give a damn any more. Let summer come, let an epidemic break out, then they'll know who they drove into exile. When are you sailing?

PETRA. (*Stepping* D. C.) You really decided to go, Father?

STOCKMANN. Absolutely. When do you sail, Captain?

HORSTER. (*Crossing* D. L. C. *to* L. *of* PETRA.) That's really what I came to talk to you about.

STOCKMANN. Why, something happen to the ship?

CATHERINE. (*Happily to* STOCKMANN.) You see! We can't go!

HORSTER. No, the ship will sail. But I won't be aboard.

STOCKMANN. No!

PETRA. You fired, too? 'Cause I was this morning!

CATHERINE. Oh, Captain, you shouldn't have given us **your** house . . .

HORSTER. Oh, I'll get another ship. It's just that the owner, Mr. Vik, happens to belong to the same party as the Mayor, and I suppose when you belong to a party and the party takes a certain position . . . Because Mr. Vik himself is a very decent man . . .

STOCKMANN. Oh, they're all decent men!

HORSTER. No, really, he's not like the others . . .

STOCKMANN. He doesn't have to be. A party is like a sausage grinder—it mashes up clear heads, longheads, fatheads, blockheads, and what comes out?—meatheads! (*Bell at* U. R. *door.* PETRA *goes to answer it.*)

CATHERINE. (*Crossing to* U. *of* R. C. *table.*) Maybe that's the glazier . . .

STOCKMANN. (*Stepping to* HORSTER.) Imagine, Captain . . . (*Pointing to door.*) He refused to come all morning. (PETER *enters* U. R. *and stands just below arch.* PETRA *stays in hall.*)

PETER. If you're busy . . .

STOCKMANN. (*Crossing to* D. *of* R. C. *table.* HORSTER *crosses* D. L. C.) Just picking up rocks and broken glass. Come in, Peter. What can I do for you this fine, brisk morning? (*He demonstratively pulls his robe tighter around his throat.*)

CATHERINE. (*Indicating dining-room.*) Come inside, won't you, Captain?

HORSTER. (*Crossing* U.) Yes. I'd like to finish our talk, Doctor.

STOCKMANN. (*Stepping* L. *a little.*) Be with you in a minute, Captain. (HORSTER *exits into dining-room, preceded by* CATHERINE *and* PETRA. PETER *says nothing, looking at the damage, he is standing* D. R.) Keep your hat on if you like, it's a little draughty in here today.

PETER. Thanks, I believe I will. (*Puts his hat on.*) I think I caught cold last night—that house was freezing.

STOCKMANN. I thought it was kind of warm—suffocating, as a matter of fact. What do you want?

PETER. May I sit down? (*Starts to sit in* R. C. *chair.*)

STOCKMANN. Not there, a piece of the solid majority . . . (*Refers to window.*) is liable to open your skull! There. (*Indicates* D. L. *chair.* PETER *crosses to* D. L. *chair, sits, while taking a large envelope out of his breast pocket.*) Now don't tell me!

PETER. Yes. (*Hands him envelope.*)

STOCKMANN. (*Gets it and sets it on table, returns, sits on* R. C. *chair.*) I'm fired.

PETER. The Board met this morning. There was nothing else to do, considering the state of public opinion. (*Pause.*)

STOCKMANN. You look scared, Peter.

PETER. I . . . haven't completely forgotten that you're still my brother.

STOCKMANN. I doubt that.

PETER. You have no practice left in this town, Thomas.

STOCKMANN. People always need a doctor.

PETER. A petition is going from house to house. Everybody is signing it. A pledge not to call you any more. I don't think a single family will dare refuse to sign it.

STOCKMANN. You started that, didn't you?

PETER. No. As a matter of fact, I think it's all gone a little too far. I never wanted to see you ruined, Thomas. This will ruin you.

STOCKMANN. No, it won't . . .

PETER. For once in your life, will you act like a responsible man?

STOCKMANN. Why don't you say it, Peter? You're afraid I'm going out of town to start publishing things about the Springs, aren't you?

PETER. I don't deny that. (*Takes off hat.*) Thomas, if you really have the good of the town at heart you can accomplish everything without damaging anybody, including yourself. (*Pause.*)

STOCKMANN. What's this now?

PETER. Let me have a signed statement saying that in your zeal to help the town, you went overboard and exaggerated—put it any way you like, just so you calm anybody who might feel nervous about the water. If you'll give me that, you've got your job, and I give you my word you can gradually make all the improvements you feel are necessary. Now that gives you what you want . . .

STOCKMANN. You're nervous, Peter.

PETER. (*He is, steps back to sofa.*) I am not nervous!

STOCKMANN. (*Rises, stands* U. C. *of* PETER.) You expect me to remain in charge while people are being poisoned?

PETER. In time you can make your changes . . .

STOCKMANN. When—five years, ten years? You know your trouble, Peter? You just don't grasp, even now, that there are certain men you can't buy.

PETER. I'm quite capable of understanding that; but you don't happen to be one of those men. (*Slight pause.*)

STOCKMANN. What do you mean by that now?

PETER. You know damned well what I mean by that. Morten Kiil is what I mean by that.

STOCKMANN. Morten Kiil?

PETER. (Rising.) Your father-in-law, Morten Kiil.

STOCKMANN. I swear, Peter, one of us is out of his mind; what are you talking about?

PETER. Now don't try to charm me with that professional innocence . . .

STOCKMANN. What are you talking about?

PETER. You don't know that your father-in-law has been running around all morning buying up stock in Kirsten Springs?

STOCKMANN. (Perplexed.) Buying up stock?

PETER. Buying up stock, every share he can lay his hands on!

STOCKMANN. Well, I don't understand, Peter, what's that got to do with . . . ?

PETER. (Crossing STOCKMANN to D. of R. C. chair in agitation, takes off hat.) Oh, come now, come now, come now . . .

STOCKMANN. (Crossing to D. of sofa.) I hate you when you do that! Don't just walk around gabbling " Come now, come now "— what the hell are you talking about?

PETER. Very well, if you insist on being dense. A man wages a relentless campaign to destroy confidence in a corporation. He even goes so far as to call a mass meeting against it. The very next morning, when people are still in a state of shock about it all, his father-in-law runs all over town picking up shares at half their value.

STOCKMANN. (After a pause.) My God!

PETER. And you have the nerve to speak to me about principles?

STOCKMANN. You mean you actually believe that I . . . ?

PETER. I'm not interested in psychology! I believe what I see! And what I see is nothing but a man doing a dirty, filthy job for Morten Kiil, and let me tell you, by tonight every man in this town'll see the same thing!

STOCKMANN. Peter, you, you . . . !

PETER. (Pointing to study door L.) Now go to your desk and write me a statement denying everything you've been saying or . . .

STOCKMANN. Peter, you're a low creature!

PETER. All right, then, you'd better get this one straight, Thomas. If you're figuring on opening another attack from out of town, keep this in mind: the morning it's published I will send out a subpoena for you and begin a prosecution for conspiracy. I've been trying to make you respectable all my life; now if you want to make the big jump there'll be nobody there to hold you back. Now do we understand each other?

STOCKMANN. Oh, we do, Peter! (KIIL *enters hall* U. R. PETER *starts for door and almost bumps into him.* STOCKMANN *crosses* U. *to* R. *of dining-room arch.*) Get the girl—what the hell is her name?—scrub the floors, wash down the walls, a pestilence has been here!

PETER. (*Turning to* STOCKMANN, *pointing to* KIIL.) Hah! (*He exits* U. R. KIIL *crosses* D. *to* R. *table, sits in* R. *chair.*)

STOCKMANN. (*Crossing* D. *to* L. *of* KIIL.) Morten, now what have you done? What's the matter with you? Do you realize what this makes me look like?! (KIIL *simply sits there, grinning up at him, takes some stock shares out of his inside coat pocket and sets them on table.* STOCKMANN *breaks off on seeing them.*) Is that . . . them?

KIIL. That's them, yes. Kirsten Springs shares. And very easy to get this morning.

STOCKMANN. Morten, don't play with me, what's this all about?

KIIL. What are you so nervous about? Can't a man buy some stock without . . . ?

STOCKMANN. (*Moves to* KIIL.) I want an explanation, Morten.

KIIL. Thomas, they hated you last night.

STOCKMANN. You don't have to tell me that.

KIIL. But they also believed you. They'd love to murder you, but they believe you. (*Slight pause.*) The way they say it, the pollution is coming down the river from Windmill Valley.

STOCKMANN. That's exactly where it's coming from.

KIIL. Yes. And that's exactly where my tannery is.

STOCKMANN. (*Sitting, slowly.*) Well, Morten, I never made a secret to you that the pollution was tannery waste.

KIIL. I'm not blaming you. It's my fault. I didn't take you seriously. But it's very serious now. Thomas, I got that tannery from my father, he got it from his father; and his father got it from my great-grandfather. I do not intend to allow my family's name to stand for the three generations of murdering angels who poisoned this town.

STOCKMANN. I've waited a long time for this talk, Morten. I don't think you can stop that from happening.

68

KIIL. No, but you can.

STOCKMANN. I?

KIIL. (*Nudging the shares.*) I've bought these shares because . . .

STOCKMANN. Morten, you've thrown your money away: the Springs are doomed.

KIIL. I never throw my money away, Thomas. These were bought with your money.

STOCKMANN. My money? What . . . ?

KIIL. You've probably suspected that I might leave a little something for Catherine and the boys?

STOCKMANN. Well, naturally, I'd hoped you'd . . .

KIIL. (*Touches shares.*) I decided this morning to invest that money in some stock, Thomas.

STOCKMANN. (*Slowly getting up. Slight indication of* CATHERINE *off* L.) You bought that junk with Catherine's money . . . !

KIIL. People call me badger, and that's an animal that roots out things, but it's also some kind of a pig, I understand. I've lived a clean man and I'm going to die clean. You're going to clean my name for me.

STOCKMANN. Morten . . .

KIIL. Now I want to see if you really belong in a strait-jacket.

STOCKMANN. How could you dare do such a thing? What's the matter with you?

KIIL. Now don't get excited, it's very simple. If you should make another investigation of the water . . .

STOCKMANN. I don't *need* another investigation, I . . .

KIIL. If you think it over and decide that you ought to change your opinion about the water . . .

STOCKMANN. But the water is poisoned, it's poisoned!

KIIL. If you simply go on insisting the water is poisoned, (*Holds up shares.*) with these in your house, then there's only one explanation for you—you are absolutely crazy!

STOCKMANN. You're right! I'm mad! I'm insane!

KIIL. (*Rising.*) You must be! You're stripping the skin off your family's back—only a madman would do a thing like that!

STOCKMANN. Morten, Morten, I'm a penniless man, why didn't you tell me before you bought this junk?

KIIL. (*Crossing to* STOCKMANN.) Because you would understand it better if I told you after. (*Holds him by lapels with terrific force.* STOCKMANN *turns his face away.*) And Goddammit, I think you

69

do understand it now! Don't you! Millions of tons of water come down that river. How do you know the day you made your tests there wasn't something unusual about the water?

STOCKMANN. (*Breaking* D. L. C.) No, I took too many samples.

KIIL. How do you know? (*Following him.*) Why couldn't those little animals have clotted up only in the patch of water you souped out of the river? How do you know the rest of it wasn't pure?

STOCKMANN. (*Crossing* KIIL *to* C. KIIL *follows.*) It's not probable . . . people were getting sick last summer . . .

KIIL. They were sick when they came here, or they wouldn't have come!

STOCKMANN. Not intestinal diseases, skin diseases . . .

KIIL. The only place anybody gets a bellyache is here?! There are no carbuncles in Norway? Maybe the food was bad! Did you even think of the food?

STOCKMANN. (*With desire to agree with him.*) No . . . I didn't look into the food . . .

KIIL. Then what the hell makes you so sure it's the water?

STOCKMANN. Because I tested the water and . . .

KIIL. (*Turning to* STOCKMANN.) Admit it. We're all alone here . . . you have some doubt . . .

STOCKMANN. (*Crossing,* U. *around table, then* L. C.) Well, nothing is a hundred percent on this earth, but . . .

KIIL. Then you have a perfect right to doubt the other way! You have a scientific right! And did you ever think of some disinfectant? I bet you never even thought of that!

STOCKMANN. Not for a mass of water like that, you can't . . .

KIIL. Everything can be killed. That's science! (*Crosses to* STOCKMANN, *turning him around.*) Thomas, I never liked your brother, you have a perfect right to hate him . . .

STOCKMANN. I didn't do it because I hate my brother!

KIIL. (*During this speech,* STOCKMANN *slowly turns to face* KIIL.) Part of it, part of it, don't deny it! You admit there's some doubt in your mind about the water, you admit there may be ways to disinfect it, and yet you went after your brother as though the only way to cure the thing was to blow up the whole Institute! There's hatred in that, boy, don't forget it. (*Crosses to* R. *table, picks up shares in* R. *hand, stands in front of* C. *chair.*) These can belong to you now, so be sure, be sure; tear the hatred out of your heart, stand naked in front of yourself—*are you sure?!*

STOCKMANN. What right have you to gamble my family's future on the strength of my convictions?

KIIL. Ah ha! Then the convictions are not really that strong!

STOCKMANN. I am ready to hang for my convictions! (*Crosses R. to* KIIL.) But no man has a right to make martyrs of others; my family is innocent. Sell back those shares, give her what belongs to her, I'm a penniless man!

KIIL. Nobody is going to say Morten Kiil wrecked this town. (*Crosses R. of R. chair, turns.*) You retract your " convictions," or these go to charity.

STOCKMANN. Everything?

KIIL. There'll be a little something for Catherine, but not much. I want my good name. It's exceedingly important to me.

STOCKMANN. (*Bitterly.*) And charity . . .

KIIL. Charity will do it, or you will do it. It's a serious thing to destroy a town.

STOCKMANN. Morten, when I look at you I swear to God I see the devil! (HOVSTAD *and* ASLAKSEN *enter* U. R. STOCKMANN *starts after* KIIL, *who retreats* U. R.) You . . . (KIIL *almost bumps into* ASLAKSEN. STOCKMANN, U. R. C., *crosses* D. *below table, then* C.)

ASLAKSEN. (*Holds up hand defensively.*) Now don't get excited, please! (HOVSTAD *and* ASLAKSEN *smile a little at* KIIL.)

KIIL. Too many intellectuals here! (*He is standing below archway* U. R.)

ASLAKSEN. (*Apologetically.*) Doctor, can we have five minutes of . . . ?

STOCKMANN. I've got nothing to say to you . . .

KIIL. I want an answer right away. You hear? I'm waiting. (*Exits* U. R.)

STOCKMANN. All right, say it quick. What do you want?

HOVSTAD. (*Crossing* D. *to* L. *of* R. C. *table,* ASLAKSEN *crossing* D. *to* R. *of* R. C. *table.*) We don't expect you to forgive our attitude at the meeting, but . . .

STOCKMANN. (*Grasping for the word.*) Your attitude was prone . . . prostrated . . . prostituted!

HOVSTAD. All right, call it whatever you want . . .

STOCKMANN. I've got a lot on my mind, so get to the point. What do you want?

ASLAKSEN. (*Crossing to* D. *of* R. C. *table.*) Doctor, you should have

71

told us what was in back of it all. You could have had the *Messenger* behind you all the way.

HOVSTAD. You'd have had public opinion with you now. Why didn't you tell us?

STOCKMANN. Look, I'm very tired. Let's not beat around the bush . . .

HOVSTAD. (*Gestures toward door where* KIIL *went out.*) He's been all over town buying up stock in the Springs. It's no secret any more.

STOCKMANN. (*Slight pause.*) Well, what about it?

HOVSTAD. (*In a friendly way.*) You don't want me to spell it out, do you?

STOCKMANN. I certainly wish you would, I . . .

HOVSTAD. All right, let's lay it on the table. Aslaksen, you want to . . . ?

ASLAKSEN. No—no, go ahead.

HOVSTAD. Doctor, in the beginning we supported you. (*Slowly, to drive it into his head.*) We couldn't go on supporting you because, in simple language, we didn't have the money to withstand the loss in circulation. You're boycotted now? Well, the paper would have been boycotted, too, if we'd stuck with you.

ASLAKSEN. You can see that, Doctor . . .

STOCKMANN. Oh, yes, but what do you want?

HOVSTAD. *The People's Messenger* can put on such a campaign that in two months you'll be hailed a hero in this town.

ASLAKSEN. (*Crossing to* R. *of* HOVSTAD.) We're ready to go.

HOVSTAD. We will prove to the public that you had to buy up the stock because the management would not make the changes required for the public health. In other words, you did it for absolutely scientific, public-spirited reasons. (*Steps to* STOCKMANN.) Now, what do you say, Doctor?

STOCKMANN. You want money from me, is that it?

ASLAKSEN. Well, now, Doctor . . .

HOVSTAD. (*To* ASLAKSEN.) No, don't walk around it. (*To* STOCKMANN.) If we started to support you again, Doctor, we'd lose circulation for a while. We'd like you—or Mr. Kiil, rather—to make up the deficit. (*Quickly, stepping to* STOCKMANN.) Now that's open and above-board and I don't see anything wrong with it. Do you? (*Pause.* STOCKMANN *looks at him, then crosses him and* ASLAKSEN *to window* R. *in thought.*)

72

ASLAKSEN. Remember, Doctor, you need the paper, you need it desperately.

STOCKMANN. (*Returns to* D. R. *of* R. *chair.*) No, there's nothing wrong with it at all. I . . . I'm not at all averse to cleaning up my name, although for myself it never was dirty. I don't *enjoy* being hated, if you know what I mean.

ASLAKSEN. Exactly.

HOVSTAD. Aslaksen, will you show him the budget? (ASLAKSEN *reaches into his pocket.*)

STOCKMANN. Just a minute. There is one point. I hate to keep repeating the same thing, but the water is poisoned.

HOVSTAD. (*Crossing* ASLAKSEN.) Now, Doctor . . .

STOCKMANN. Just a minute. The Mayor says that he will levy a tax on everybody to pay for the reconstruction. I assume you are ready to support that tax at the same time you're supporting me?

ASLAKSEN. That tax would be extremely unpopular.

HOVSTAD. Doctor, with you back in charge of the baths as Medical Officer, I have absolutely no fear that anything can go wrong . . .

STOCKMANN. In other words, you will clean up my name so that I can be in charge of the Corruption.

HOVSTAD. But we can't tackle everything at once. A new tax, there'd be an uproar!

ASLAKSEN. It would ruin the paper!

STOCKMANN. Then you don't intend to do anything about the water?

HOVSTAD. We have faith you won't let anyone get sick!

STOCKMANN. In other words, gentlemen, you are looking for someone to blackmail into paying your printing bill.

HOVSTAD. (*Indignantly.*) We are trying to clear your name, Doctor Stockmann! And if you refuse to cooperate, if that's going to be your attitude . . .

STOCKMANN. Yes? Go on. What will you do?

HOVSTAD. (*Taking* ASLAKSEN'S R. *arm, starts to cross* STOCKMANN.) I think we'd better go.

STOCKMANN. (*Steps* D. *into their way.*) What will you do? I would like you to tell me! Me, the man two minutes ago you were going to make into a hero—what will you do now that I won't pay you!

ASLAKSEN. Doctor, the public is almost hysterical!

STOCKMANN. To my face, tell me what you are going to do!

HOVSTAD. The Mayor will prosecute you for conspiracy to destroy a corporation, and without a paper behind you, you will end up in prison!

STOCKMANN. And you'll support him, won't you?! I want it from your mouth, Hovstad! This little victory you will not deny me. (HOVSTAD *crosses* STOCKMANN, *starts for* U. R. *door.* STOCKMANN *takes his* R. *arm, stops him.*) Tell the hero, Hovstad; you're going to go on crucifying the hero, are you not? Say it to me . . . you will not leave here until I get this from your mouth!

HOVSTAD. (*Stepping back, looking directly at him.*) You are a madman. You are insane with egotism, and don't excuse it with humanitarian slogans, because a man who'll drag his family through a lifetime of disgrace is a demon in his heart! (*Advances on* STOCKMANN.) You hear me? A demon who cares more for the purity of a public bath than the lives of his wife and children. Doctor Stockmann, you deserve everything you're going to get! (HOVSTAD *starts to go* U. R. STOCKMANN *is struck by his ferocious conviction.* ASLAKSEN *comes toward him, taking budget out of his pocket.*)

EJLIF. (*Off* R.) Mother!

ASLAKSEN. (*Nervously.*) Doctor, please, consider it; it won't take much money and in two months' time I promise you your whole life will change and . . .

EJLIF. (*Entering hall* U. R.) Mother! Mother!

CATHERINE. (*Without shawl, running to front door* U. R. *from dining-room behind bookcase.*) What happened? My God, what's the matter? (STOCKMANN, *alarmed, crosses* U. *as* CATHERINE *brings* MORTEN *down, followed by* EJLIF. PETRA *and* HORSTER *enter* U. R.; *she crosses* D. C.; *he crosses* D. L. C.; HOVSTAD *with* ASLAKSEN *on his* R. *give to* L. C.) Something happened! Look at him!

MORTEN. I'm all right. It's nothin'.

STOCKMANN. (*Very much the doctor.*) What happened here?

MORTEN. Nothin', Papa, I swear . . .

STOCKMAN. (*To* EJLIF.) What happened? Why aren't you in school?

EJLIF. The teacher said we better stay home the rest of the week.

STOCKMAN. The boys hit him?

EJLIF. They started calling you names so he got sore and began to fight with one kid and all of a sudden the whole bunch of them jumped on him.

CATHERINE. (*To* MORTEN.) Why did you answer?

MORTEN. (*Indignantly, to* STOCKMANN.) They called him a traitor! (*To* EJLIF.) My father is no traitor!

EJLIF. But you didn't have to answer!

CATHERINE. (*Pushing* EJLIF *away a little.*) You should've known they'd all jump on you! They could have killed you!

MORTEN. I don't care!

STOCKMANN. (*To quiet him—and his own heart.*) Morten . . .

MORTEN. (*Pulls away from* STOCKMANN.) I'll kill them! I'll take a rock and the next time I see one of them I'll kill him! (STOCKMANN *reaches for* MORTEN *who, thinking he will be chastised, starts to pull away.* STOCKMANN *catches him and starts gripping him against his chest.*) Let me go! Let me . . .

STOCKMANN. Morten . . . Morten . . . (MORTEN *cries in his arms.*)

MORTEN. They called you traitor, an enemy . . . (*He sobs.*)

STOCKMANN. Sssh. That's all. Wash your face. (*Turns to* ASLAKSEN *and* HOVSTAD.) Good day, gentlemen.

HOVSTAD. Let us know what you decide, and we'll . . .

STOCKMANN. I've decided. I am an enemy of the people . . .

CATHERINE. Tom, what are you saying?

STOCKMANN. To such people who teach their own children to think with their fists—to them I'm an enemy! And my boy . . . my boys . . . my family . . . I think you can count us all enemies!

ASLAKSEN. Doctor, you could have everything you want . . .

STOCKMANN. Except the truth. I could have everything but that. The water is poisoned.

HOVSTAD. But you'll be in charge . . .

STOCKMANN. But the children are poisoned, the people are poisoned! If the only way I can be a friend of the people is to take charge of that corruption, then I am an enemy! The water is poisoned, poisoned, poisoned, that's the beginning of it and that's the end of it! Now get out of here!

HOVSTAD. You know where you're going to end?

STOCKMANN. (*Taking umbrella from* ASLAKSEN.) I said get out of here! (HOVSTAD *and* ASLAKSEN *cross* STOCKMANN *and the boys.* CATHERINE *and the boys cross* U. C. *around* R. *table.* PETRA *crosses* R. *to* STOCKMANN. HOVSTAD *crosses* D. L. C.)

CATHERINE. What are you doing?

ASLAKSEN. You're a fanatic! You're out of your mind!

75

CATHERINE. What are you doing?

STOCKMANN. They want me to buy the paper, the public, the pollution of the Springs, buy the whole pollution of this town. They'll make a hero out of me for that! (*Furiously to* ASLAKSEN *and* HOVSTAD.) But I am not a hero, I am the enemy and now you're first going to find out what kind of enemy I am! I will sharpen my pen like a dagger—you, all you "friends" of the people are going to bleed before I'm done! Go, tell them to sign the petitions, warn them not to call me when they're sick; beat up my children; and never let her . . . (*Points to* PETRA.) in the school again or she'll destroy the immaculate purity of the vacuum there! See to the barricades, the truth is coming, ring the bells, sound the alarm! The truth, the truth is out, and soon it will be prowling like a lion in the streets!

HOVSTAD. Doctor, you're out of your mind. (*He and* ASLAKSEN *turn* U. R. *to go quickly.* STOCKMANN *runs after them.*)

STOCKMANN. Out of here, out of here!

EJLIF. (*Rushing at them.*) Don't you say that to him!

STOCKMANN. (*At ball.*) Out of here! (*He throws umbrella after them, slams the door* U. R. *behind them, crosses* C. *with* EJLIF *on his* R. *After a moment:*) I've had all the ambassadors of hell to-day, but there'll be no more. Now, now listen, Catherine. Children, listen. We are besieged. They'll call for blood now, they'll whip the people like oxen . . . (*A rock comes through remaining pane of* R. *window.* MORTEN *starts for window.* STOCKMANN *stops him.* HORSTER *turns to face* STOCKMANN.) Stay away from there!

CATHERINE. The Captain knows where we can get a ship . . .

STOCKMANN. No ships!

PETRA. We're staying?

CATHERINE. But they can't go back to school, I won't let them out of the house!

STOCKMANN. We're staying.

PETRA. Good!

STOCKMANN. We must be careful now. We must live through this. Boys, no more school. I'm going to teach you. And Petra will. Do you know any kids, street louts, hookey-players . . . ?

EJLIF. Oh, sure!

STOCKMANN. We'll want about twelve of them to start. But I want

76

them good and ignorant, absolutely uncivilized. Can we use your house, Captain!

HORSTER. Sure, I'm never there.

STOCKMANN. Fine! We'll begin, Petra, and we'll turn out not taxpayers and newspaper subscribers, but free and independent people, hungry for the truth. Oh, I forgot! Petra, run to Grandpa and tell him . . . tell him . . . as follows . . . NO!

CATHERINE. (*Puzzled.*) What do you mean?

STOCKMANN. It means, my dear, that we are all alone. And there'll be a long night before it's day . . . (*A rock smashes through another window.* PETRA *starts for window,* STOCKMANN *holds her back.* HORSTER *crosses to* D. *of window, crouches low and looks out.*)

HORSTER. Half the town is out. (STOCKMANN *pulls family down low. All are crouching a little.*)

CATHERINE. What's going to happen? Tom! What's going to happen? (HORSTER *crosses* D. R. C., *looks* U. *at family.*)

STOCKMANN. I don't know. But remember now, everybody. You are fighting for the truth, and that's why you're alone. And that makes you strong—we're the strongest people in the world . . . (*Crowd noises build.*) And the strong must learn to be lonely.

CURTAIN

PROPERTY LIST

ACT I—SCENE 1

Magazine rack with magazines D. R.
  On it: Vase of flowers
Potted plants in window bay
Toy hook-and-ladder fire truck in window bay
Light tan curtains in bay windows
Brown drapes over window, U. R. entrance, dining room arch
Round-topped table R. C.
  On it: Kerosene lamp, bowl of apples, tobacco humidor, ashtray with
    matches
One armchair R. of round-topped table
One armchair L. of round-topped table
Very large bookcase against back wall of room
  In it: Books of all sizes and colors, microscope on C. shelf, odd in-
    strument on C. shelf
Two-place sofa L. C.
  On it: Two matching pillows
Long table behind sofa (same length as sofa)
  On it: Photo album, bowl of almonds—unshelled, bowl of red
    berries and green leaves, ashtray with matches
Porcelain tile stove U. L.
  Downstage of it: Basket of wood, fire tongs, poker
Brocade armchair D. L.
Small footstool downstage of armchair
  On it: Basket of knitting with knitting needles
Floor lamp upstage of D. L. armchair
In dining room U. L.: Buffet against back wall of dining-room, dining-
    room table set for supper: beef, bread, etc., four dining-room
    chairs grouped around table, chandelier hanging over table
Picture on D. R. wall
Diploma on U. R. wall
Picture on U. L. wall
Library steps against bookcase U. C.

ACT I—SCENE 2

Strike: Toddy tray, pot, bottles, cups, pipe, knitting, fruit and nut
    bowls, all coats and hats except Stockmann's
Close dining-room portieres

Act II—Scene 1

Rolltop desk u. r.
  On it: Stockmann's manuscript, ledger, standing on edge on down-
    stage end of desk, various papers, letters, etc.
Office chair for desk
Waste-basket down-stage of desk
Long table l. c.
  On it: Large scrapbook, newspaper clippings, scissors, measuring
    sticks, mug of glue
Straight chair at head of table, stage c.
Straight chair at c. of table
Kerosene lamp on r. wall above desk
Kerosene lamp on d. l. wall
Picture of King above desk
Map of city on wall u. c.

Act II—Scene 2

Platform of crates r. c.
Smaller crates, forming steps at l. of platform
Small crate d. l. of platform
On platform: Straight chair at r., small table at c.
Two straight chairs at r. of platform
Wooden chest d. l.
High-backed chair d. l.
Wall lamp upstage of r. door
Wall lamp in u. l. corner
Ship model on shelf on u. c. wall

Act III

Same as Act I except: Flowers are struck, potted plants and toy in
  window bay are overturned, upstage window pane is broken, rocks
  are placed: One d. c., two under r. c. chair, one under r. chair,
  one in front of window, six piled on table, downstage curtain out
  of tieback

OFFSTAGE PROPERTY TABLES

Up Left:
Toddy tray, pot of water, 5 cups (Catherine, Act I—Scene 1)
Tan manila envelope (Catherine, Act I—Scene 1)
Personal note (Catherine, Act I—Scene 1)
Glass of milk (Petra, Act I—Scene 2)
Brown manuscript, two pages (Peter, Act II—Scene 1)

Cloth bag containing raisins (Child, Act II—Scene 2)
Cigars, pipes, tobacco, matches (Crowd, Act II—Scene 2)
Prop baby in blanket (Hedvig, Act II—Scene 2)
Down Left:
Cigar box with 3 unwrapped, punctured cigars (Ejlif, Act I—Scene 1)
Pipe, half-filled with tobacco (Morten, Act I—Scene 1)
Doctor's manuscript with 5 pages (Petra, Act I—Scene 1)
Up Right:
Set of four textbooks strapped together; in top book is sealed post-
   marked business letter (Petra, Act I—Scene 1)
One business-size addressed letter, sealed (Catherine, Act III)
Composition book (Petra, Act III)
One business-size unsealed letter (Peter, Act III)
One packet of ten stock shares (Kiil, Act III)
Doorbell
Down Right:
Tray with pitcher, three glasses glued to it
Three rocks
Glass crash

TODAY'S HOTTEST NEW PLAYS

☐ **MOLLY SWEENEY by Brian Friel, Tony Award-Winning Author of** *Dancing at Lughnasa.* Told in the form of monologues by three related characters, *Molly Sweeney* is mellifluous, Irish storytelling at its dramatic best. Blind since birth, Molly recounts the effects of an eye operation that was intended to restore her sight but which has unexpected and tragic consequences. *"Brian Friel has been recognized as Ireland's greatest living playwright. Molly Sweeney confirms that Mr. Friel still writes like a dream. Rich with rapturous poetry and the music of rising and falling emotions...Rarely has Mr. Friel written with such intoxicating specificity about scents, colors and contours."* - New York Times. [2M, 1W]

☐ **SWINGING ON A STAR (The Johnny Burke Musical) by Michael Leeds. 1996 Tony Award Nominee for Best Musical.** The fabulous songs of Johnny Burke are perfectly represented here in a series of scenes jumping from a 1920s Chicago speakeasy to a World War II USO Show and on through the romantic high jinks of the Bob Hope/Bing Crosby "Road Movies." Musical numbers include such favorites as "Pennies from Heaven," "Misty," "Ain't It a Shame About Mame," "Like Someone in Love," and, of course, the Academy Award winning title song, "Swinging on a Star." *"A WINNER. YOU'LL HAVE A BALL!"* - New York Post. *"A dazzling, toe-tapping, finger-snapping delight!"* - ABC Radio Network. *"Johnny Burke wrote his songs with moonbeams!"* - New York Times. [3M, 4W]

☐ **THE MONOGAMIST by Christopher Kyle.** Infidelity and mid-life anxiety force a forty-something poet to reevaluate his 60s values in a late 80s world. *"THE BEST COMEDY OF THE SEASON. Trenchant, dark and jagged. Newcomer Christopher Kyle is a playwright whose social satire comes with a nasty, ripping edge - Molière by way of Joe Orton."* - Variety. *"By far the most stimulating playwright I've encountered in many a buffaloed moon."* - New York Magazine. *"Smart, funny, articulate and wisely touched with rue...the script radiates a bright, bold energy."* - The Village Voice. [2M, 3W]

☐ **DURANG/DURANG by Christopher Durang.** These cutting parodies of *The Glass Menagerie* and *A Lie of the Mind,* along with the other short plays in the collection, prove once and for all that Christopher Durang is our theater's unequivocal master of outrageous comedy. *"The fine art of parody has returned to theater in a production you can sink your teeth and mind into, while also laughing like an idiot."* - New York Times. *"If you need a break from serious drama, the place to go is Christopher Durang's silly, funny, over-the-top sketches."* - TheatreWeek. [3M, 4W, flexible casting]

DRAMATISTS PLAY SERVICE, INC.
440 Park Avenue South, New York, New York 10016 212-683-8960 Fax 212-213-1539

TODAY'S HOTTEST NEW PLAYS

❏ **THREE VIEWINGS by Jeffrey Hatcher.** Three comic-dramatic monologues, set in a midwestern funeral parlor, interweave as they explore the ways we grieve, remember, and move on. *"Finally, what we have been waiting for: a new, true, idiosyncratic voice in the theater. And don't tell me you hate monologues; you can't hate them more than I do. But these are much more: windows into the deep of each speaker's fascinating, paradoxical, unique soul, and windows out into a gallery of surrounding people, into hilarious and horrific coincidences and conjunctions, into the whole dirty but irresistible business of living in this damnable but spellbinding place we presume to call the world."* - New York Magazine. [1M, 2W]

❏ **HAVING OUR SAY by Emily Mann.** The Delany Sisters' Bestselling Memoir is now one of Broadway's Best-Loved Plays! Having lived over one hundred years apiece, Bessie and Sadie Delany have plenty to say, and their story is not simply African-American history or women's history...it is our history as a nation. *"The most provocative and entertaining family play to reach Broadway in a long time."* - New York Times. *"Fascinating, marvelous, moving and forceful."* - Associated Press. [2W]

❏ **THE YOUNG MAN FROM ATLANTA Winner of the 1995 Pulitzer Prize. by Horton Foote.** An older couple attempts to recover from the suicide death of their only son, but the menacing truth of why he died, and what a certain Young Man from Atlanta had to do with it, keeps them from the peace they so desperately need. *"Foote ladles on character and period nuances with a density unparalleled in any living playwright."* - NY Newsday. [5M, 4W]

❏ **SIMPATICO by Sam Shepard.** Years ago, two men organized a horse racing scam. Now, years later, the plot backfires against the ringleader when his partner decides to come out of hiding. *"Mr. Shepard writing at his distinctive, savage best."* - New York Times. [3M, 3W]

❏ **MOONLIGHT by Harold Pinter.** The love-hate relationship between a dying man and his family is the subject of Harold Pinter's first full-length play since *Betrayal*. *"Pinter works the language as a master pianist works the keyboard."* - New York Post. [4M, 2W, 1G]

❏ **SYLVIA by A.R. Gurney.** This romantic comedy, the funniest to come along in years, tells the story of a twenty-two year old marriage on the rocks, and of Sylvia, the dog who turns it all around. *"A delicious and dizzy new comedy."* - New York Times. *"FETCHING! I hope it runs longer than Cats!"* - New York Daily News. [2M, 2W]

DRAMATISTS PLAY SERVICE, INC.
440 Park Avenue South, New York, New York 10016 212-683-8960 Fax 212-213-1539